HOLLYWOOD DISH!

Recipes
& Tales of
Tips & Tales of
Hollywood
Caterer
Recipes
Tips & Tales of

foreword by Elizabeth Taylor
food photography by Tom Paul

HOLLYWOOD DISH!

Recipes, Tips & Tales of a Hollywood Caterer

by Nick Grippo with Jane C. Russo

ANGEL CITY PRESS

Dedication

To Elizabeth Taylor,
Carrie Fisher and Cindy Williams
for their caring and candor.

ANGEL CITY PRESS, INC.
2118 Wilshire Boulevard, Suite 880
Santa Monica, California 90403
(310) 395-9982
http://www.angelcitypress.com

First published in 1998 by Angel City Press
1 3 5 7 9 10 8 6 4 2
FIRST EDITION

ISBN 1-883318-09-2

Hollywood Dish!
By Nick Grippo with Jane C. Russo
Copyright © 1998 Nick Grippo and Jane C. Russo

Designed by Dave Matli
Food photography by Tom Paul

Distributed to the book trade by Universe Publishing through St. Martin's Press, 175 Fifth Avenue, New York NY 10010

Printed in Hong Kong

Library of Congress Cataloging-in-Publication Data

Grippo, Nick
       Hollywood dish! : recipes, tips, and tales of a Hollywood caterer / by Nick Grippo with Jane C. Russo ; food
          photography by Tom Paul. – 1st ed.
               128 p. ; ill. ; 20 cm.
               Includes bibliographical references and index.
               ISBN 1-883318-09-2 (cloth)
               1. Cookery. 2. Celebrities — California — Los Angeles — Anecdotes. 3. Hollywood (Los
Angeles, Calif.) — Social life and customs — Anecdotes. I. Title
TX714.G765 1998
641.5 21   98-25356
                                       CIP

Foreword

Life is a journey. If we're lucky, we experience it accompanied by good friends and good food. Both play an important role in helping us celebrate the good times, console us during the bad, and simply enhance the joy of everyday living. When it comes to food and friendship, Nick Grippo immediately comes to mind. Nick and I have spent a lot of time together over the years, and a lot of that time was spent eating . . . and eating. And it was all delicious. I'm especially fond of his Caesar Salad with Homemade Parmesan Croutons. Throughout the years his cooking has always pleased my family and guests. He's someone I can always count on.

I'm glad he can recall the recipes for you.
I hope you enjoy them as much as I have.

Elizabeth Taylor

contents

Introduction

Food means many things to me. It's hard to think of a holiday or occasion when food doesn't come to my mind. Birthdays, weddings, funerals, festivals . . . even *fasting* . . . make me think of food and being with friends. Food is the eternal relationship. In sickness and in health, till death do us part . . . we literally can't live without it! But when some people think about the actual preparation, cooking and serving of food (not to mention *cleaning up)*, many think "fear." Even celebrities.

What a great paradox! We want the togetherness and the conviviality that's centered around sharing food with family and friends. But many of us lack the time, energy, interest or confidence to do the cooking ourselves.

That's where I come in. I'm a caterer. I love all things associated with food. But it took me a while to realize I could make it my life's work.

I came to Hollywood over thirty years ago. Like so many others, I had my heart set on show business. I studied acting with fellow students including Ted Danson, Michelle Pfeiffer, Patrick Swayze, Cindy Williams, John Larroquette and Donna Mills. I appeared in many plays and produced and directed some very forgettable films. Looking back now, I know what I liked best about those days. It was cooking for my friends. We'd cheer up each other when we were out of work (often) and toast our successes (getting one line in a burger commercial). The conclusion of every production was ritually celebrated with a fabulous wrap party that I would prepare.

During those days I had a marvelous penthouse atop a wonderful vintage Hollywood mansion with a spectacular 360-degree view of Los Angeles. With its warm European flavor of marbled floors, high-beamed ceilings and lush tropical decor, it became a retreat of sorts, where friends could come for a comforting meal. Guests enjoyed my interpretations of my Italian mother's recipes. These little suppers gradually grew into fabulous dinner parties. When the film business proved to be more anxiety-ridden than rewarding, I focused my energies on the one thing that always gave me the most pleasure – carefully crafting and serving cuisine. My home became a private dining salon where I'd host exclusive parties for Hollywood's elite. Notables and show biz insiders were delighted with this unique environment for their power pow-wows. In time I realized I was more of a success at putting together these evenings than at theater work or films – and I guess others felt the same. I got more calls to produce dinner parties than I received to produce plays.

Like most good things, the word spread. I found myself expanding (I'm not talking about my waistline – that would come later) and began catering private dinners for stars like Elizabeth Taylor, wrap parties for feature films like Steven Spielberg's *E.T.*, romantic weddings (including Cindy Williams's), birthday parties for celebrities like Harrison Ford and Ed Begley, Jr., Thanksgiving dinner for Barry Manilow, Christmas for Ted Danson and virtually every very special (and not-so special) occasion imaginable. I even catered a tea party for Patrick Swayze's Arabian horse – and a mere 2,500 guests!

As my catering business grew, many people asked, "How did you *make* this?" My answer was to issue a monthly newsletter and to conduct private cooking classes, both of which I continue to this day. I'd create the menu or teach a specifically requested dish. (*Look who's directing whom!)* Often it would be a group experience with a few close friends, and we'd make an evening of it. We'd spend hours in the kitchen preparing and comparing who's seeing whom, who's buying what and who's going where (sound familiar?). Then we'd enjoy our scrumptious efforts with invited friends and mates. What fun we had!

I've had some especially memorable classes with Hollywood's contemporary Perle Mesta, Carrie Fisher. There was no telling which stars would cross her threshold and be transformed into a cooking student! Never did I imagine I'd be feeding Meryl Streep, Robin Williams, Richard Dreyfuss, Woody Harrelson, Angelica Huston and Barbra Streisand from Carrie's kitchen.

I don't know anyone who hasn't wanted to learn a new recipe that he or she can absolutely depend on. Because let's face it: Cooking can be scary. Who isn't unnerved at the thought of cooking dinner for your spouse's family, your boss or a new love? Haven't you ever wanted to crawl under the table after a guest points to something on the plate asking, "What's *that?*" and then banishes it to a napkin once you've identified the mystery food. And who hasn't wanted to dial 911 at just the *thought* of cleaning up? Whether it's for your in-laws, your in-loves, your friends or even a foe, you want your efforts to be a success.

Having catered several thousand parties, I think that cooking is a lot like acting and producing. It requires good materials (the best ingredients are just as important as the best dialogue). It demands preparation. It calls for careful rehearsals (I would never make a new dish for an event without first trying it out). Once we know our "lines," we can improvise. Yet cooking and entertaining mean more than just preparing food. It's about art direction: mixing the right colors and textures on the plate and much, much more. It's about knowing how to make food substitutions for guests with special needs or for you when you've run out of an ingredient. It's also about cleanup. It's about being super-organized! But most important, it's about giving and getting good directions.

This book, like my newsletter, is written for people who want to prepare dishes easily and confidently so they can enjoy themselves when they entertain. Just like incomes, some recipes are richer than others (we can't count calories and fat grams every second, can we?) while others are leaner and lighter. Some recipes are unbelievably simple, while others are complex.

This book is also for those curious souls who want to know the inside story about what I have prepared for many stars in Hollywood, so they can cook the same recipes for the real stars in their own lives. There are tips, observations, recollections and revelations mixed in. But, if you're looking for dirt, better get a book on landscaping.

Creating cuisine is my favorite thing in life. I have especially loved providing it for the people on the following pages, because I admire and respect *their* work. They've inspired me with their talents and I only hope I've done a culinary version of the same for them.

So to those who've honored me by enjoying my food and to those who've entrusted me with their special occasions, I say thank you. And to you new friends about to share my offerings – ENJOY!

– Nick Grippo, Hollywood 1998

menus

I love cooking for any occasion. But no matter the size of the gathering, there are many factors to consider before finalizing a menu. I ask a lot of questions and you should, too: What's the occasion? Formal or not? Indoors or out? Stand-up or sit-down? Location? How much time is available for the festivities? What's the budget?

Besides those logistical questions, the most important thing to consider is your vision for the event. Will the party be old friends, or a chance for all to make new friends? Is it an annual event such as a birthday, or a special occasion such as a baby shower or graduation? Is there a traditional dish that must be included, such as a turkey or a birthday cake? Having these answers will help you plan your menu.

Once I have determined the kind of party I'm planning, what to serve evolves very naturally. Spending time with your guests is often your first priority. If so, avoid the complicated dishes that demand last-minute attention. And if time is a factor, forget about serving your favorite eight-course meal. Save that for a sit-down evening with ample time. I love the relaxed atmosphere of dining with friends, so I serve family style. Or, if it's a big group, buffet style. I like to involve old friends and new in some part of the meal preparation. I try to make it fun — so, as an example, I'll ask my guests to take turns shaking a glass jar filled with fresh cream. After thirty minutes of shaking, it turns into fresh butter. At big parties, I set up individual serving stations to give guests an opportunity to meet others while filling their plates. If it's a standup party, I never serve food that requires more than a fork — finger food is best. And for holiday parties, I incorporate natural objects that define the season: Easter eggs, pumpkins, fall leaves, gourds, holly. There's nothing like a holiday table decorated with fresh fir boughs and holly. If space is a problem, I create different levels on the buffet table to make more room for the food; it's dramatic and it's easy to reach.

On the next few pages is a sampling of menus from some memorable gatherings. All the recipes are included with a few exceptions that I will now justify (we cooks always try to justify *why* we didn't make *everything!* I can't help it). I have yet to come across a ham equal to the taste of HoneyBaked Ham, nor one easier to serve since it's spiral sliced. I certainly can't duplicate the taste or cut of this ham whether it's warmed in the oven for a dinner party or served buffet style at room temperature. (These wonderful, succulent hams are available by mail-order from HoneyBaked Hams by calling 800-854-5995.) In the same way, although I enjoy baking very much and often prepare the desserts for my parties, there are occasions that require certain items for which I defer to the best pastry chef or bakery I can find. And I recommend that you do the same. My favorite bakery for bread is Brown's Bakery in North Hollywood, California. They'll ship their products, so if you don't have a favorite baker near you, you can turn to my best source. And when it comes to pastry, I choose the ultimate Swiss pastry artisan, Emil. Emil's Swiss Pastry in Los Angeles produces French-style custards and pastries. My wedding cake guru is Jaqki of Jaqki's Cake Creations in North Hollywood — but I know, it's next-to-impossible to ship a wedding cake (though it has been done!), so you'll find a place near you and get the best of the best. Be certain to taste before ordering at any bakery!

When planning a menu for the stars in your life, my advice is to always read a new recipe twice, don't be afraid to experiment, allow yourself the necessary time for preparation and take advantage of the best local resources that you have. That way, you insure that your party will be a complete success.

INTRODUCTION TEA

Assorted Tea Sandwiches on Multicolored Bread
Fresh Strawberries and Raspberries
Ginger Scones with Jelly and Crème Fraîche
Blueberry Cobbler
Mom's Greek Butter Cookies
Chocolate-dipped Coconut Macaroons
Key Lime Pie
Carrot Cake with Cream Cheese Frosting
Miniature Custard Fruit Tarts
Miniature Eclairs and Napoleons

Tea and Coffee Service
Lemon and Cloves
Cream and Sugar

THANKSGIVING-CHRISTMAS DINNER

Baked Brie with Baguettes
Country Pâté
Spinach Dip presented in Red Cabbage surrounded by Carrots, Celery,
   Cherry Tomatoes, Green Onions and Artichoke Hearts

Garden Salad Garnished with Hearts of Palm
Oven-roasted Turkey with Corn Bread, Sausage and Mushroom Stuffing
Sweet Potatoes in Orange Skins
Creamed Onions
Mashed Potatoes and Gravy
Cranberry, Shallot and Dried-Cherry Compote
Assorted Relishes with Radishes, Celery and Carrot Sticks

Pumpkin Pie with Whipped Cream on the Side
Pear Mincemeat Pie

Coffee and Tea Service

CHRISTMAS DINNER

Red Pepper, Coriander and Sun-dried Tomato Dip
Brandied Gravlax
Marinated Shrimp
Marinated Artichokes
Marinated Mushrooms
Assorted Olives
Pâté with Mushrooms and Pistachios
Salmon Walnut Pâté
Italian and French Cheeses
Breadsticks
Fresh Fruits and Berries
Assorted Breads and Biscuits

Caesar Salad with Parmesan Croutons
Prime Rib of Beef with Porcini Pan Gravy and Horseradish Sauce
Yorkshire Pudding
HoneyBaked Ham
Risotto Milanese
Old-Fashioned Potatoes Gratin
Pureed Carrots in Lime-Green Squash
French Rolls with Sweet Butter

Crème Brûlée
Pecan Pie
Pumpkin Pie
Fruitcake
Gingerbread House
Orange-Chocolate Truffles

Espresso Bar

NEW YEAR'S EVE PARTY

Prosciutto-wrapped Figs
Sliced Melons and Papayas
Marinated Artichokes
Rigatoni with Broccoli and Tomato in Pesto Sauce
Assorted Olives
Fresh Winter Berries
Italian Cheeses
Assorted Breads and Breadsticks

Japanese Tempura with Assorted Vegetables including Yams, Mushrooms,
    Onions, Green Onions, Green Beans, Zucchini and Eggplant
Orange Roughy Tempura
Tamari Ginger Sauce

Apple Tarte Tatin
Mango-Lime Mousse
Flambé Berries

Espresso Bar

WRAP PARTY

STATION #1 – Crudités
Carrot Sticks, Celery Sticks, Broccoli Buds, Cherry Tomatoes, Mushrooms
    complemented with Olive Tapanade and Spinach Dip
Nachos
Assorted Cheeses including New York Cheddar, Jarlsberg, Strawberry Cream
    Cheese, Brie, and Saga Blue
Assorted Breads and Crackers
Chicken Satay
A cascading display of Fresh Fruit including Honeydew, Cantaloupe,
    Watermelon, Pineapple, Grapes, Raspberries and Kiwi

STATION #2 – Tempura Bar
Chef-Prepared Tempura featuring Shrimp, Cod and Sea Bass
    Yams, Mushrooms, Red Onions, Green Onions, Broccoli, Green Beans,
    Zucchini, Snap Peas, Cauliflower and Eggplant
Tamari-Ginger Sauce
Sliced Fresh Ginger

STATION #3 – Quesadilla Bar
Chef-prepared Quesadillas with choice of Chopped Chiles, Sliced Green
    and Black Olives, Sliced Green Onions, Grated Monterey Jack Cheese,
    Jalapeño Chilies, Avocado
Guacamole
Fresh Tomato Salsa
Sour Cream

Chocolate Layer Cake

Coffee and Tea Service

FUND-RAISER

Assorted Cheeses including Jarlsberg, New York Cheddar and Brie
Crackers and Assorted Breads

Garden Salad with Sherry Vinaigrette
Pasta Primavera, Pasta Carbonara, and Pasta Puttanesca prepared from
   Imported Capellini, Fusilli and Spaghetti Pastas
Garlic Bread
Moussaka

Assorted Sherbets
Chocolate Layer Cake
Green Grapes with Brown Sugar and Crème Fraîche

Coffee and Tea Service

BIRTHDAY DINNER

Spanakopeta

Mushroom-Chive Salad with Red Wine Vinaigrette
Classic California Pasta Salad
Belgian Endive with Fresh Herbs
Poached Salmon with Dill Sauce
Stuffed Breast of Veal
Braised Broccoli in Tomato Cups
Assorted Breads and Rolls with Butter

Coconut Angel Food Cake

Coffee and Tea Service

hosted by ReneeTaylor

hosted by HarrisonFord

FOURTH of JULY BARBECUE

hosted by Elizabeth Taylor with special guest Nancy Reagan

Crudités of Assorted Fresh Vegetables with Red Pepper, Coriander and Sun-dried Tomato Dip
Marinated Shrimp
Assorted Cheeses
Homemade Tostadas
Mango Salsa, Fresh Tomato Salsa and Guacamole
Nachos
Tropical Fruits and Berries
Spicy Nuts
Deviled Eggs
Breads, Crackers and Toasts

Rodeo Drive Ribs
Hamburgers
Haute Dogs, plain and with Bacon and Cheese
Turkey Dogs
Fried Chicken
Old-Fashioned Potato Salad
Caesar Salad with Parmesan Croutons
Greek Salad
Beer-baked Beans
Caprese Salad
Assorted Rolls and Buns with Butter

Strawberry Shortcake

Coffee and Tea Service

WEDDING BUFFET LUNCHEON

hosted by Marjorie Lord Volk

Crudités including Carrot Rounds, Celery Sticks, Zucchini Rounds, Cauliflower Buds, Broccoli Buds, Green Pepper Rings, Cherry Tomatoes complemented with Spinach Dip

Honeydew
Cantaloupe
Strawberries
Pineapple

Chicken Piccata with Lemon Slices, Capers and Marsala Wine Sauce
Grilled Swordfish with Basil Butter
Garden Salad with Sherry Vinaigrette
French Rolls and Sweet Butter

Wedding Cake with Fresh Berries

Coffee and Tea Service

OPENING ACTS!

c h a p t e r 2

An appetizer is like a good first kiss: It leaves you wanting more. In some respect, appetizers are like actors, coming in all shapes, sizes and temperaments. Some of them need tremendous attention before they can make their big entrance. Others require little or no advance preparation and are just naturally beautiful and delicious. The trick in deciding on appetizers is to choose the hors d'oeuvres that will complement your meal while also allowing you to enjoy your evening. Cold appetizers, prepared in advance, permit you more time to spend with your guests, while hot ones are more time-consuming. Appetizers like finger foods, which do not require a knife and fork, mean you'll have fewer plates and less cutlery to clean afterward.

Generally speaking, the rule in choosing appetizers is much like casting a film. You want a variety of characters that will provide major contrast yet complement one another. Extravagant appetizers that are rich in texture and taste such as Chicken Satay best complement a simpler main course. A vegetable crudité platter will prepare the palate for a dinner rich with sauces or gravies, such as Steak au Poivre or Tenderloin of Beef with Madeira Sauce.

Next to always using the freshest ingredients possible, my general rule of thumb is to serve in abundance two or three appetizers (too many will detract from what is to follow) unless you're having a party of nothing but appetizers. Presentation, or "staging" as I think of it, is also important in that no matter how delicious your offerings, they first must look inviting. Before that first kiss, you know there has to be some attraction, and that is simply the result of good presentation. I like food arranged at different heights, so they're not laid out flat like a hospital tray. I love serving cheese and crackers in pretty baskets; hollowed-out cabbage heads hold dips beautifully. I especially like large planks of wood, white china platters and simple, elegant bowls that are uncluttered in design and ornamentation. The food is the focus.

Chapter Two

In the Clouds

I've been enamored of Elizabeth Taylor since childhood. I couldn't pass a newsstand without buying a magazine with her picture on the cover. When I was a teenager, I took a date to see *Cat on a Hot Tin Roof*. I was instantly mesmerized by the twenty-foot image of grace and beauty before me. Sitting transfixed on the edge of my seat for the entire movie, I completely forgot I had a date and violated the teen ritual of putting my arm around her. She never spoke to me again.

As a young, naive, independent filmmaker in Los Angeles, I would confidently boast of my ability to work with anyone. There wasn't an actor alive I would hesitate to direct. Except, of course, Elizabeth Taylor. She was the only person I openly conceded would intimidate me.

In Hollywood, everyone knows somebody famous. Chances are you'll never *meet* that celebrity, but you might hear about them. As it happened, my friend Arthur Bruckell was Elizabeth's hairdresser. In 1973 my wife and I had just separated and Arthur, wanting to cheer me up, suggested a trip to Mexico. Distraught over my impending divorce and missing my young son terribly, I was fraught with ambivalence. But Arthur intimated that Elizabeth and Richard Burton would be in Mexico on a romantic sojourn and promised to introduce me. I agreed to go and we left on a Sunday.

Crudités can be prepared in advance and served plain or with dips. In addition to being healthful, they make a beautiful presentation when arranged with some care and creativity. I love to serve them resting on a bed of kale, parsley, or any colorful leafy greens in season. They're great in baskets surrounding a dip served in a hollowed-out squash or arranged on a decorative platter. The bonus in serving them is that they're not filling and what's left over can be used the next day in a salad, steamed, or used in preparing another dish.

Whenever possible, I use "baby" vegetables that can be found in many fine markets. These miniature varieties, although usually pricier than regular vegetables, are always tender and because of their size require less preparation. For example, baby carrots just need to be scrubbed well and a little of the green top left on for color.

CRUDITÉS

radishes
broccoli florets
mushrooms
green, red, yellow and orange pepper spears
celery
carrots
blanched snow peas
zucchini
fennel hearts
jicama
cherry tomatoes
yellow pear tomatoes
young asparagus spears
green beans
green onions

cucumbers, seeded and half peeled
cauliflower florets
yellow squash

Clean, trim and cut into bite-size pieces any or all the above vegetables in advance of serving. Radishes, celery, fennel, scallions, carrots and jicama and green beans can all be stored individually in cold water in airtight containers overnight in your refrigerator. All other vegetables can be stored dry in airtight plastic bags and refrigerated. Prior to serving, arrange attractively in a basket or on a platter of your choice. ✎

Just after boarding the plane, it was announced that takeoff would be inexplicably delayed. Drinks were served again and *again*. Sometime between the third and fourth drink, Arthur confirmed that Elizabeth would indeed be flying to Mexico later in the week and that Tuesday was her birthday.

The *thought* of meeting her gave me goose bumps! She'd been my dream girl ever since *National Velvet*! Although I was somewhat bleary-eyed, the thought of meeting her triggered the nervous reaction of looking at the window to check my reflection, smooth down a hair, straighten my collar . . . when out of the window I saw a black limousine crawl onto the runway, right up to our plane! Who gets door-to-door jet service? You're right! It was Elizabeth and Richard, ahead of schedule.

Just then Arthur drolly noted I'd be meeting them sooner than expected and he got up to say hello.

On that particular airline there was no first-class section. The prestige seats were the first row immediately behind the pilot. In full view of every passenger, it's the aeronautical equivalent of center stage. Starring in those seats was now the most famous couple in the world.

After takeoff, Arthur returned and commanded me to get up to be introduced. Paralyzed with intimidation, I wondered if I could even walk straight. Arthur coaxed me as I stumbled up the aisle, eight miles high. While the clouds rushed by I thought I must be in heaven for I was greeted by the most beautiful violet eyes I had ever seen.

As Elizabeth extended her hand, I gushed that I had dreamt of meeting her my entire life and never thought it would be so wonderful. Looking me straight in the eye she quickly quipped that I probably never expected to be so high! And she wasn't referring to the altitude! She zinged me right then and there!

Elizabeth explained that she and Richard needed some R&R and the quaint fishing port of Puerto Vallarta had become a favorite spot ever since Richard filmed *Night of the Iguana* there. Elizabeth inquired where we were staying and much to my surprise, Arthur replied that we were uncertain.

Elizabeth insisted that we stay at her guest house.

Could this be happening to me? An independent filmmaker of *no* acclaim staying with Elizabeth Taylor and Richard Burton at their villa in Mexico? *Si, Si.*

This vacation was much needed by all. Arthur had permed one too many heads. I was afraid I'd never see my infant son again. Elizabeth was recovering from surgery and Richard said that he had just completed an alcohol recovery program. Their stormy relationship was somewhat strained and they arrived in Mexico needing to heal both physical and emotional wounds.

Richard's recovery did not last the length of the flight. He was inconsolable and preferred to stay by himself. Elizabeth, on the other hand, was very determined to have a nice vacation. In Richard's absence, Arthur and I became her companions for walks on the beach, ocean swims and endless conversation. My five-day visit extended to ten. And while the trip and my marriage ultimately ended, that time marked the

RED PEPPER, CORIANDER and SUN-DRIED TOMATO DIP
Makes 2 ½ cups

2 7-ounce jars roasted red peppers, well drained
3 ounces sun-dried tomatoes (dried, not in oil, soaked in hot water for 5 minutes, drained well, reserving 3 tablespoons soaking liquid)
2 garlic cloves, minced
1 ½ teaspoons ground cumin
1 or 2 bottled pickled jalapeño chiles, seeded and minced (wear rubber gloves)
1 teaspoon fresh lemon juice
¼ cup chopped fresh coriander
½ cup chopped green onions, whites only
4 ounces cream cheese, softened to room temperature

1) In a food processor, puree the red peppers, tomatoes, garlic, cumin, jalapeños, lemon juice, coriander and green onions until the mixture is smooth.

2) Add the cream cheese in pieces, salt to taste and puree the mixture, adding some of the reserved tomato liquid to thin the dip to the desired consistency, being sure to scrape down the sides of the bowl occasionally.

3) To serve, transfer to a hollowed-out spaghetti squash surrounded by crudités and/or tortilla chips. ✑

This is a very hearty dip ideal for vegetable crudités. It also works well with grilled fish. As soon as I take the fish off the coals and prior to serving, I spread a tablespoon of Tapenade across the fish making a dramatic accent that underscores its flavor.

OLIVE TAPENADE DIP
Makes 2 cups

8 ounces pitted black olives (preferably Kalamatas)
1 7-ounce can albacore tuna, packed in oil and drained
¼ cup capers, rinsed and drained
¼ cup fresh lemon juice
1 tablespoon dark rum, or to taste
1 large garlic clove
½ cup olive oil
freshly ground black pepper

19

1) Combine first 6 ingredients in a food processor or blender until smooth.

2) Add the olive oil in a slow stream, blending thoroughly. Season to taste with pepper. Serve with crudités. ✑

No individuals watch their weight more closely than my celebrity clients. This favorite recipe and most requested appetizer has been "lightened up" on many occasions by using nonfat sour cream, nonfat mayonnaise and nonfat cream cheese. The soup mix, garlic and dill make it spicy and satisfying, so if you like thick, creamy dips, you won't even notice the difference! Here's the original recipe.

SPINACH DIP
Makes 10-12 servings

16-ounces cream cheese (regular or nonfat)
1 cup mayonnaise (regular or nonfat)
2 cups sour cream (regular or nonfat)
2 packets Lipton Onion Soup Mix
½ teaspoon garlic powder
2 tablespoons chopped fresh dill
20 ounces frozen chopped spinach, thawed, drained and squeezed dry

1) In a blender, mix the cream cheese, sour cream and mayonnaise.

2) Add the soup mix and seasoning and blend again.

3) Remove from blender to a serving bowl. Gently stir in the spinach. Pour into hollowed-out round bread or cabbage and serve with assorted crudités. ✎

This recipe is a staple at all my parties. It's almost a trademark. I pass the nuts as hors d'oeuvres, I put them at the bar, I bring them as gifts to dinner parties, at interviews with new clients and I always include them in my gift baskets. I've made this recipe using walnuts, pecans, hazelnuts and cashews, but the almonds are my favorite. I call them the "Nuts from Hell" because they are spicy, addicting and difficult to make. So be warned!

SPICY ALMONDS
Serves 6

3 tablespoons peanut oil
2 cups whole blanched almonds
½ cup sugar
1½ teaspoons salt
1½ teaspoons ground cumin
1 teaspoon hot pepper flakes
1 tablespoon sugar

1) Heat the oil in a heavy-bottomed frying pan over medium-high heat. Add the almonds and ½ cup of the sugar. Stir until the almonds become golden and the sugar caramelizes.

2) Remove the almonds from the pan and toss in a bowl with the salt, cumin, pepper flakes and the 1 tablespoon of the sugar.

3) Empty the nuts onto a cookie sheet and, using 2 forks, separate each nut as they cool. Be careful not to touch them with your fingers, because the caramel can burn. Do this carefully but quickly or you'll end up with almond brittle! ✎

beginning of a friendship that has lasted over twenty-five years.

When I left the film business and started my catering company, Elizabeth was one of my biggest supporters. She's flown me to exotic spots and had me cater parties for professional and personal occasions. I've cooked many Thanksgiving, Easter and Christmas dinners at her home as well as having been a guest at her table for many celebrations.

It's funny to think that the one "star" who kept me in awe has become a dear friend. This brilliantly talented actress is someone I've also come to admire for her courage, candor and caring for those not only near to her, but for the millions of people who look to her as an agent of hope in curing AIDS. Indeed, many, many scenes and players have changed in our lives over the years, yet one thing has remained unchanged. I am still that same devoted fan. ✎

spicyalmonds

HarrisonFord
Elizabeth
JohnnyMathis
DannyDeVito&RheaPearlman

A Master Craftsman

Shortly after his *Star Wars* success, Harrison Ford called me for a small family birthday party for his father, Chris. At the time he lived in Beverly Hills on Braeridge Road off Benedict Canyon Drive.

Harrison's house was near the horseback riding paths developed in the 1920s by the Beverly Hills Bridle Path Association. Made up of prominent local residents including Will Rogers, the paths were created not to promote riding, but to beautify what was considered an ugly strip of land along Sunset Boulevard and Rodeo Drive. Every aspect of the Beverly Hills community had to be beautiful – it was the top priority of the developers and residents. And the eyesore along Sunset had to be fixed! So with meticulous attention, riding paths were created with hedges of flowering shrubs on both sides of its entire length. The bridle trail continued to Doheny Drive, and at Benedict Canyon Drive it connected with a web of trails up into the mountains. The beautification project fostered new interest in the equestrian sport and became a choice destination for tourists.

Harrison's house would have impressed those Beverly Hills founders with its outstanding craftsmanship and decor. If those trails that ran by his house were used today, I could easily imagine people nodding their heads in approval as they trotted by. Or aggressive tourists curbing their horses and ringing the bell to ask for a look. It was one of the most perfectly detailed homes I have ever seen and certainly inspired me. Everywhere were beautiful handwoven rugs and Craftsman-style furniture.

Using fresh spinach makes all the difference in this recipe. Don't shy away from it because it's difficult to wash. Place the spinach in a basin filled with fresh water. Holding the stems, remove the spinach a few leaves at a time, letting the water and sand drain down into your basin. Cut off all the stems. Replace basin with fresh water and repeat the process. Pat the leaves dry.

SPANAKOPETA
(CHEESE and SPINACH PIE)
Serves 10 to 15

3 pounds fresh spinach
12 green onions, including tops, finely chopped
1 cup virgin olive oil
½ cup parsley leaves, minced
8 large eggs, beaten well
l teaspoon fresh dill, minced
1 pound imported Danish feta cheese
salt
½ pound filo sheets
1 cup (2 sticks) butter, melted

To make a large pie to be cut into diamonds:

1) Preheat oven to 350°F. Wash and completely dry the spinach leaves. Remove the stems and coarsely chop leaves.

2) Sauté the onions in ½ cup olive oil until tender. Add the spinach, parsley, beaten eggs, dill, cheese and the cooked green onions. Salt lightly and mix well.

3) Butter a 9x13-inch baking pan and line with 5 sheets of filo, brushing each one with the melted butter combined with ½ cup olive oil. Keep the remaining filo dough sheets covered with a damp cloth.

4) Spread the spinach mixture on top and place the remaining sheets of filo on top of the spinach mixture. Again, brush each one with the butter and oil. Brush the top sheet with the butter/oil mixture and cut into 3-inch diamonds with a very sharp knife.

5) Bake for 45 minutes. Lightly recut and serve hot or cold as an appetizer or side dish.

To make individual triangles:

1) Place 1 sheet of filo dough on a flat surface and brush with melted butter.

2) Cut the sheet in 3 even strips lengthwise.

3) Spoon a tablespoon of spinach mixture onto the end of each strip (keeping the remaining strips covered with a damp towel) and form a triangle by folding right-hand corner to opposite end, like a flag. Continue folding until entire strip is used. Repeat until all the mixture is used.

4) Place triangles on a buttered baking sheet. Brush with melted butter and bake until puffy and golden brown, about 10 minutes.

The triangles can be covered and stored in the refrigerator up to 2 days before baking. ✑

STUFFED MUSHROOMS
Serves 4

8 large mushroom caps, stems removed and
   finely chopped
¼ cup (½ stick) butter
3 tablespoons minced shallots
½ cup diced walnuts
½ cup breadcrumbs
¼ teaspoon thyme
salt and freshly ground black pepper
¼ cup (½ stick) melted butter for dipping the
   mushroom caps

1) Preheat oven to 350°F. Butter a baking dish.

2) Melt butter in a medium-sized skillet over medium-high heat. Add shallots and sauté until wilted. Add nuts and chopped stems and cook 2 minutes.

3) Mix in breadcrumbs, thyme and salt and pepper to taste.

4) Dip mushroom caps in melted butter and fill with breadcrumb mixture, brush tops with melted butter. Place in baking dish and bake until thoroughly heated, about 10-12 minutes. ✑

baked **Brie**

BAKED BRIE
Serves 10 to 12

1 2.2-pound wheel of brie (60% butterfat)
   trimmed of the top rind only, leaving the
   creamy cheese exposed
1 cup light brown sugar, packed
1 cup slivered almonds, toasted

1) Preheat oven to 350°F.

2) Remove the brie from the wooden box. Line
the bottom portion of the box with aluminum
foil so it can withstand the oven heat. Replace
the brie in the lined bottom portion of the box
with exposed cheese facing up. Put the box on a
baking sheet.

3) Firmly pack the sugar on the top of brie and
sprinkle it with the nuts.

4) Bake until the sugar starts to melt and the
cheese is hot and runny (about 15 to 20 minutes).

5) Serve with cheese knives and sliced baguettes. ✓

DEVILED EGGS
Serves 12 to 24

12 hard-cooked eggs
greens for garnish
3 green onions, finely chopped, whites only
2 tablespoons Dijon-style mustard
½ cup Mayonnaise (pg. 89)
¼ cup chopped fresh dill
¼ teaspoon cumin
4 tablespoons unsalted butter
¼ teaspoon cayenne pepper
salt and pepper to taste

Warm and absolutely unpretentious, Harrison took great pride in the house he shared with his future wife, screenwriter Melissa Mathison. He had worked on the house extensively. He was a master craftsman who had supported himself as a carpenter for many years prior to his stardom. In fact, I remember someone telling me at a party that an incredible guy named Harrison had made a magnificent brick path at the Laurel Canyon home of record producer Paul Rothschild.

In addition to a wonderful wooden stairwell, his house had an outdoor rock shower area that could be seen only from

1) Add eggs to boiling water and cook for 20 minutes or until hard cooked. Cool the eggs in cold water and peel. Cut in half lengthwise.

2) Scoop out the yolks and set the whites aside on a bed of greens.

3) Add all other ingredients to the egg yolks and mash thoroughly with an electric beater until smooth. Season to taste.

4) Place the yolk mixture in a pastry bag with a star tip and fill egg whites. Garnish with any of the following ingredients: caviar, chopped ham, fresh dill or chervil.

If you don't have a pastry bag you can fill the egg whites by using a teaspoon dipped into water before you scoop to prevent sticking. Smooth with a butter knife or use a serrated knife to create a pattern. ✓

the glass door in the master bedroom. It reminded me of a grotto waterfall where Dorothy Lamour could have rinsed her long tresses in the glistening stream that gushed from the rocks.

In the movie business, the people who provide food for the cast and crew are called "craft services." Looking at all of Harrison's beautifully made woodwork, I remember thinking that we both were craftsmen. I hoped just then that his dad would find my cooking as pleasing as I found his son's house — a dinner with ingredients as equally fine as the materials used to build this home. Not realizing he was within earshot, I remarked to one of my assistants that it was *almost* a perfect house. No sooner had I said this than a voice from around the corner inquisitively asked what *would* make it perfect. Harrison had heard me! Not knowing whether to be embarrassed or flattered, I paused to collect myself and suggested larger kitchen doors to provide a more expansive and dramatic entrance for serving in the dining room. For just like actors, a caterer's efforts need good sets and great lighting.

Harrison listened intently. He liked my idea of stringing lanterns above the patio where the party food was served. In fact, he devised a system to hang them so we wouldn't make holes in the wood.

With Harrison's help, dinner was beautifully lit as well as delicious. Needless to say I was extremely pleased when sometime later he and Melissa asked me to cater the cast party for a film Melissa had written. It had been a closely guarded secret in Hollywood. The movie was most often referred to by the initials *E.T.* ✓

Tea sandwiches, although time-consuming to prepare, offer endless opportunities to mix and match a variety of food ingredients while exercising your creativity. I like to offer tea sandwiches both open-face and closed. Tea sandwiches made with whimsical cookie cutters and filled with traditional stuffings (like peanut butter and jelly, or a mild cheese) are especially popular with kids.

TEA SANDWICHES

An assortment of thinly sliced breads:

Egg bread, white, wheat, pumpernickel, whole grain and any of the new multicolored, herbed and nut breads currently on the market.

Spread with:

Mustard Dill Sauce, pg.41
Cranberry Mayonnaise, pg. 89
Anchovy Mayonnaise, pg.89
Mustard Mayonnaise, pg.89
sweet butter at room temperature, whole mayonnaise or stone ground mustard

Top or stuff with:

Brandied Gravlax, pg.41
Marinated Shrimp, pg.29
Country Pâté, pg.38
Pâté with Mushrooms and Pistachios, pg.39
Eggplant Oriental, pg.30
Salmon Walnut Pâté, pg.41
or smoked turkey, watercress, crumbled bacon, Japanese or red radishes, sprouts or chives, yellow and red cherry tomatoes, sliced egg, sliced green or black olives, flat-leaf, Italian parsley, fresh dill and capers

To assemble:

1) Trim the crusts from the breads. Using your favorite cookie cutter or a serrated knife, cut the bread into interesting shapes, rounds, rectangles, squares or triangles. Use a damp tea towel to cover the bread to prevent it from drying out.

2) Spread one side of the bread with a little butter, top that with your choice of smoked turkey, watercress, radishes, sprouts, chives, tomatoes, sliced eggs or any combination you fancy. Top with another piece of bread spread with plain or flavored mayonnaise.

Some of my favorite closed tea sandwiches are: Gravlax with Mustard Dill Sauce with a sprig of dill; smoked turkey with Cranberry Mayonnaise; tomato, cucumber and watercress with Anchovy Mayonnaise with chopped chives; Salmon Walnut Pâté with watercress or parsley leaves; and Country Pâté with sliced green olives.

Open-face sandwiches I enjoy are Brandied Gravlax or Marinated Shrimp with Mustard Dill Sauce or Mustard Mayonnaise spread with almost any garnish. The pâtés don't require any butter – just garnish. ✓

HONEY RIBLETS
Makes about 50 hors d'oeuvres

3½ pounds pork spareribs, halved crosswise and cut into individual ribs
½ cup honey
¼ cup soy sauce
1 large garlic clove, minced and mashed to a paste with ¼ teaspoon salt
⅓ cup hoisin sauce
½ teaspoon English-style dry mustard
¼ cup distilled white vinegar
freshly ground black pepper to taste
greens for garnish

1) In a kettle of boiling salted water, simmer the ribs covered for 30 minutes, then drain well.

2) In a bowl, whisk together the honey, soy sauce, garlic, hoisin sauce, mustard, vinegar and black pepper. Toss the ribs in the mixture to coat them thoroughly. Cover and marinate, chilled, for at least 2 hours or overnight.

3) Arrange the riblets in 1 layer on the oiled rack of a foil-lined broiler pan and broil them about 4 inches from the heat for 3 minutes, basting frequently with the marinade. Turn and broil for 2 to 3 minutes more until they are browned and glazed. Serve on a bed of greens. ✓

Nick's Tip! Brown's Bakery at 12805 Victory Blvd. in North Hollywood, California, makes a festive multicolored bread that I often use. Available by special order, so visit them or call 818-766-3258 – they ship!

The King of Makeout

If your hormones were awake in the 1950s, you probably fell in love to a romantic Johnny Mathis song. I sure did. Whenever I hear "It's Not for Me to Say" I think of Chicago and Theresa. We'd neck for hours with Johnny singing wistfully in the background. His mellow voice was an aphrodisiac. Sometimes I think Theresa was fantasizing about Johnny while she was kissing me. But it didn't matter. She was in my arms thanks to the "King of Makeout." What a singer.

In 1992 I got a call from the *Vicki!* TV show. A Christmas week program was being put together and Johnny Mathis was one of the guests. Producer Bonny Tiegle explained that Johnny would be sharing the eggplant recipe he serves for company. I was asked to prepare it for the show.

When celebrities cook on television programs, the final dish is always prepared beforehand. This is done as a safety measure because most dishes take too long to bake in the time segment allotted. In addition, I also prepare a display of ingredients showing the food at various stages. This makes it simple for the guest to demonstrate and explain while the cameras roll.

Just before the afternoon rehearsal, I was introduced to Johnny. I was very excited to meet him. I actually wanted to say "thank you" for all those moments with Theresa! Instead I reminded him that we had met years before in Chicago when he had just recorded the soundtrack to the film *Wild Is the Wind*. The song had climbed to the top of the charts just as the film was about to open in theatres. To

marinated shrimp

MARINATED SHRIMP
Makes 12 hors d'oeuvres

1 pound jumbo shrimp (about 12 per pound),
   cooked, fresh or frozen
½ cup red wine vinegar
½ cup olive oil
2 tablespoons lemon juice
1 bunch fresh dill, cleaned of tough stems,
   coarsely chopped
6 large pimiento-stuffed green olives, coarsely
   chopped
l medium white onion, finely diced

1) Peel and devein the cooked shrimp, leaving
the tails on.

2) Combine the vinegar, oil, lemon juice and dill
in a mixing bowl. Add shrimp, toss, and add olives
and onion. Marinate for 3-4 hours covered in the
refrigerator. Serve chilled on a bed of greens. ✒

*Prosciutto with almost any of your favorite fruit in
season makes an exotically delicious starter for any
summer meal. The saltiness of this favorite ham is
contrasted with the sweet fruit, making a light and classic
opening act.*

PROSCIUTTO AND FIGS
Serves 6 to 8

12 wafer-thin slices of premium prosciutto
6 ripe kadota figs
mint for garnish

Cut figs in half lengthwise down the middle
and wrap a slice of prosciutto around it. Serve
on a platter of greens, garnished with mint. ✒

MARINATED MUSHROOMS
Serves 12 to 15

½ cup olive oil
⅓ cup lemon juice
1 sprig fresh thyme (½ teaspoon dried)
1 sprig fresh fennel (¼ teaspoon fennel seeds)
1 garlic clove, slivered
1 celery stalk, minced
10 black peppercorns
1 bay leaf
½ cup water
2 pounds small fresh white button mushrooms
½ fresh lemon
2 tablespoons finely chopped parsley

1) Combine all ingredients except the
mushrooms, lemon and parsley in a saucepan.
Bring to a boil, cover and simmer 5 minutes.

2) Meanwhile, trim the stems from the
mushrooms and rub caps with the lemon half.
Add mushrooms to the mixture in the saucepan;
simmer another 5 minutes.

3) With a slotted spoon, remove the mushrooms
from the pan and arrange them on a serving
dish. Boil the liquid in the pan until it is thick
and reduced by half. Pour the sauce over the
mushrooms and chill until ready to serve.

Serve as an appetizer sprinkled with chopped
parsley or as a salad on a bed of chilled lettuce. ✒

heighten awareness of the movie, special
advance screenings in major cities were
held with Johnny Mathis as special guest
star. Chicago went wild with the news that
Mathis would be in town. Theresa and I
flipped when we learned *our* class was
attending the screening!

It was my first celebrity encounter and
incredibly exciting! After the film (which
was fabulous) we asked him all kinds of
ridiculous questions. We'd raise our hands
and say anything, just to be able to say he
spoke to us. And God, was he polite. Not at
all snobby, considering how brilliantly his
star was shining.

So now, here I am, backstage on a TV set,
face-to-face with the man who made us
melt with songs like "Misty," "Chances
Are," "The Twelfth of Never," "A Certain
Smile" and so many others.

As mild-mannered and as youthful then
as now, Johnny candidly explained the
eggplant I prepared was a favorite recipe
he makes often. I offered him a taste and
he liked it. Just then Vicki, who's a big
"sampler," came by and tasted it too. Two
thumbs up for Nick! Whew.

I usually don't ask anything from the
people I work with. The experience and the
memories are enough. But seeing him
again that day awakened the Chicago
teenager in me. And this kid wanted a
memento. Bashful, I asked Johnny if he'd
send me a photo. Much to my delight,
several days later an autographed picture
arrived by mail. That afternoon I framed it
and hung it over the shelf that holds my
high-school yearbook, wondering what
Theresa would say. ✒

*To tell you the truth, much to my Italian parents'
chagrin, eggplant was never a favorite of mine. In fact, I
hadn't tasted it in years until Johnny's recipe. Much to
my surprise, I liked it very much and know you will too.*

EGGPLANT ORIENTAL
Serves 12 as a starter, 6 as a salad

2 eggplants, each weighing approximately 1
   pound
½ cup olive or canola oil
1 medium onion, minced
2 garlic cloves, minced
⅓ cup parsley, minced
2 green peppers, seeded, membranes removed,
   finely chopped
1 28-ounce can Italian-style tomatoes, mashed
3 tablespoons tomato paste
1 teaspoon dried basil
½ to 1 teaspoon dried oregano
½ to 1 teaspoon ground coriander
1½ teaspoons salt
½ teaspoon freshly ground black pepper
3 tablespoons ketchup
3 tablespoons chili sauce
lemon slices and assorted vegetables for garnish

1) Preheat oven to 350°F. Trim and peel
eggplants and then cut into 1-inch cubes.

2) Place eggplant cubes in a large oiled baking
pan. Bake for about 45 minutes or until soft,
stirring frequently.

3) While eggplant is baking, make the sauce.

Heat the oil in a large 4-quart heavy saucepan.
Add onion, garlic and parsley and cook over
medium heat for 5 to 7 minutes, or until soft,
stirring constantly.

4) Add peppers and cook for 3 more minutes.
Add mashed tomatoes, tomato paste, basil,
oregano, coriander, salt and pepper. Mix well
and cook covered over low heat for 20 to 30
minutes, stirring frequently.

5) Very finely chop eggplant, or process in a
food processor.

6) Add chopped eggplant to tomato sauce and cook
covered over low heat for 20 to 30 minutes more,
stirring frequently. Remove from heat and cool.

7) Stir in ketchup and chili sauce and mix well.
Taste, adding salt or pepper as needed. Chill
thoroughly.

8) To serve, transfer eggplant to a deep serving
dish lined with salad greens, or on individual
plates lined with a lettuce leaf. Garnish with
lemon slices, carrot curls, cherry tomatoes, black
olives, and green onions. ✐

MARINATED ARTICHOKES
WITH OLIVES
Serves 15

8 small fresh artichokes
1 tablespoon tarragon vinegar
1 tablespoon rice wine vinegar

salt to taste
1 teaspoon freshly ground black pepper
1 clove garlic, crushed
juice of ½ lemon
¼ cup olive oil
½ cup vegetable oil
8 bay leaves
1 lemon, thinly sliced
16 small black olives

1) Steam the artichokes for 8 to 10 minutes, or
until the heart is easily pierced with a knife. Cut
each artichoke into quarters.

2) Combine the vinegars, salt, pepper, garlic,
lemon juice and oils and pour over the
artichokes. Add the bay leaves, lemon slices and
olives and toss well. Marinate 4 hours, or
overnight. ✐

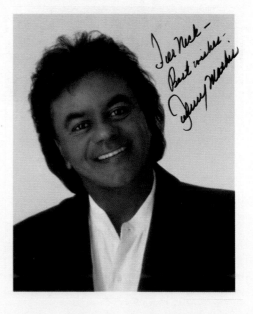

Recycle or Die

Paper or plastic? Never. No exceptions anytime, anyplace, anywhere. Not if you're cooking for Ed Begley, Jr., the fine actor and environmental champion of champions. We've had this understanding for a long time, way before he amassed his impressive list of TV and film credits or his Golden Globe Award for his portrayal of Dr. Victor Ehrlich on the Emmy Award-winning television series *St. Elsewhere*.

When I first met him he was Ed Begley, Jr., standup comic. Ed's father was a highly regarded character actor who had received the 1962 Academy Award for Best Supporting Actor in *Sweet Bird of Youth*. Known as one of Hollywood's second generation, Ed was following in his father's footsteps and just getting started. It was 1969 and Cindy Williams was a friend and devoted fan of Ed. Cindy and I were in acting class together at Los Angeles City College. One night after class, she drove us to The Ice House, the Pasadena club famous for launching many talents. Dressed in a policeman's uniform, Ed was hilarious. But it wasn't funny a few weeks later when he did the routine at another club, ran out to his car to get a prop, and was arrested for impersonating an officer. Consequently, he spent the weekend in jail. I've always found his humor, well, (excuse the pun) arresting.

I don't know if it's from our mutual parochial school experience, his sense of the absurd, or his unique perception of

Afraid to make ethnic food? Of course you can! And you can take a shortcut by looking in the poultry department for fajita strips or chicken tenders, strips of chicken already boned and skinned. You'll only have to cut it into bite-size pieces. Go for it!

CHICKEN SATAY
Serves 4

1 tablespoon unsalted butter
1 teaspoon sesame oil
1 tablespoon peanut oil
1 clove garlic, minced
1 teaspoon ginger root, minced
1 whole chicken breast halved, skinned, boned
   and cut into bite-size pieces
crushed red pepper to taste
1 tablespoon lemon juice
½ cup chicken stock
3 green onions, cleaned, coarsely chopped white
   parts only, reserving the green parts for garnish
3 tablespoons soy sauce
3 tablespoons peanut butter (smooth or chunky)
bamboo skewers (available in Asian markets)
1 tablespoon toasted sesame seeds

1) Combine butter and oils and heat in a heavy-bottomed skillet. Add garlic and ginger and saute only until soft.

2) Add the chicken and red pepper. Cook over medium heat, turning the chicken until it is white and cooked through. Add the lemon juice and chicken stock and simmer for 3 minutes. Add the onions and soy sauce. Bring mixture to a boil and remove from heat. Immediately fold in the peanut butter to form a smooth sauce.

3) Mince reserved green onion parts. Attach 1 or 2 pieces of chicken to the bamboo skewers. Place skewers in a fan-like shape in the center of a platter lined with lettuce. Garnish with toasted sesame seeds and minced green onions.

the universe that connects me to him. All I know is that he makes me laugh and think unlike anyone else. Ed is the ultimate champion of environmental conservation and will go to any length to prove his point. He bikes, uses solar energy and mass transit, reuses and recycles almost everything. To defend his position on recycling, he once accepted a challenge from a newspaper writer to fit a week's worth of household trash into the little glove compartment of his 1991 Volkswagen. Much to the amazement of everyone and with the help of a good kick, everything was squished into the tiny compartment. Point proved.

A man who practices what he preaches and serves on many environmental commissions, Ed drives an electric car that emits no pollution. I distinctly remember discovering Ed's dedication while catering a party for Cindy. Our work area extended from her kitchen into her garage, which had numerous electrical outlets. Ed drove up and extended his hand to me. Assuming it was a handshake, I was surprised to realize he was handing me an electric cord for his car which needed to be recharged. I've plugged in a lot of appliances in my day, but never a car!

Ed incorporates his environmental concern into everything, even his birthdays: Every year he hosts a party for two to three hundred friends and rather than accept gifts, encourages donations to one of his causes. One year his birthday cake was inscribed "For Earth's Sake, Vote November 3."

Over the years I've catered at least a

dozen roller-skating birthday parties for Ed and look forward to them especially because you never know whom you'll see cavorting on roller skates! Roseanne, Billy Crystal, John Tesh, Sally Kellerman, Amy Irving, Blythe Danner, Rob Lowe, Buck Henry, Cindy Williams (of course), Charles Grodin and Timothy Dalton are just some of the people who have whizzed by me!

One of my favorite Ed-isms is "Recycle or die." He was the first person I ever heard say it, way before it was popular. As a result, the phrase naturally has impacted my work. Ed insists I rent dishes and flatware for all his parties, because he won't permit any plastic (it's not bio-degradable) or paper products (spare the trees). Any leftover food is donated to a shelter; nothing is to be thrown out.

To my delight, Ed is almost as devoted to good food as he is to the environment. He's insistent about the appetizers, for instance. They must include my Chicken Satay, a combination of peanuts and chicken. Always a hit, it's the one dish Ed asked for every year *and* it is the first appetizer I ever served as a caterer. I present it surrounded by fresh vegetables so the sauce can be used as a dip as well. Easier to make than you might imagine, Chicken Satay is an exquisitely tasty departure from more traditional starters. ✑

Tempura is a very festive dish that lends itself to a beautiful display at a party. Almost any ingredient you like can be dipped in the batter, deep-fried and served. My recipe for batter is below, but you can pick up very good batters at any Asian market. Shrimp and any fish fillet (I like cod, sea bass, snapper, orange roughy and halibut) cut into 1-inch pieces also work well.

VEGETABLE TEMPURA with TAMARI-GINGER SAUCE

Batter
Makes enough batter for 2 cups of food

1⅓ cups all-purpose flour
1 teaspoon salt
¼ teaspoon freshly ground black pepper
1½ tablespoons melted butter
2 beaten egg yolks
¾ cup beer
2 egg whites
peanut oil for deep frying

1) In a mixing bowl, combine the flour, salt, pepper, butter and egg yolks. Gradually add the beer. Cover the batter and refrigerate 4 to 10 hours. Beat the 2 egg whites to stiff peaks and add them just before using the batter.

2) In a deep fryer or a large kettle with a flat bottom, heat 4 cups of oil to 350°F.

3) With tongs, dip vegetables into batter and carefully drop them into the hot oil. Fry until brown, puff up and rise to the surface.

4) Drain on paper towels and serve immediately with sauce for dipping.

Vegetables
broccoli florets
red onion rings sliced ¼-inch thick
peeled yams sliced ¼-inch thick
whole green onions
cauliflower florets
Chinese or Japanese eggplant sliced ¼-inch thick
whole green beans or snap peas, trimmed
mushrooms
zucchini, sliced ¼-inch thick

Sauce
½ cup tamari (available at Asian markets)
½ cup water
1 tablespoon dry sherry or Chinese rice wine
1 tablespoon grated fresh ginger
½ cup minced green onions, white parts only
1 small clove minced garlic
2 teaspoons sesame oil

In a bowl, whisk together all the ingredients, let stand 20 minutes and serve. This can be made in advance, covered and refrigerated. ✑

33

stuffed **Cheeese** **Quesadillas**

These are a sensational party item provided you can make and serve them immediately. Ideal for a kitchen party, this Mexican equivalent to our grilled cheese sandwich works well stuffed with almost any food including cooked shrimp, marinated eggplant, smoked turkey, or chicken breast.

STUFFED CHEESE QUESADILLAS
Makes 18 pie-shaped wedges

6 6-inch flour or corn tortillas
1½ cups grated Monterey Jack cheese
1 tablespoon vegetable oil plus additional oil for grilling
Plus your choice of condiments:
chopped chilies
sliced green and black olives
sliced green onions
jalapeño chilies
avocado
fresh cilantro leaves
black beans

Accompaniments
Guacamole, pg.36
Fresh Tomato Salsa, pg.36
Mango Salsa, pg. 36
sour cream

1) On a large griddle or in a heavy skillet, heat a tablespoon of oil over moderately high heat until hot but not smoking. Spread a tortilla on the skillet and in the middle of the tortilla, arrange the condiments of your choice and top with ¼ cup of cheese topped with another tortilla. Press down with a spatula until the cheese is melted.

Carefully turn the quesadilla over and cook until golden brown on both sides.

2) Transfer quesadilla to paper towels to drain. Cut into 6 equal wedges and serve immediately with accompaniments. Cook the remaining tortillas in the same manner, adding oil as necessary. ✎

This recipe affords another opportunity to sharpen your Asian cooking skills. Surprisingly delicious, this can easily be prepared in advance.

COLD ORIENTAL NOODLES with PEANUT SAUCE
Serves 6

Sauce

6 large garlic cloves
2 tablespoons chopped peeled fresh gingerroot
1½ cups chopped fresh cilantro (about 1 large bunch)
1 tablespoon peanut oil
1 tablespoon Oriental sesame oil
1 tablespoon hot chili oil (available at Asian markets)
½ cup smooth, unsweetened peanut butter
½ cup soy sauce or to taste
3 tablespoons sugar
3 tablespoons rice vinegar, or to taste

1) In a food processor mince the garlic with the ginger root and the cilantro.

2) Add to the above the oils, peanut butter, soy sauce, sugar and vinegar and blend well. (If a thinner sauce is desired, stir in hot water to desired consistency.) The sauce keeps for one month, covered and chilled.

Noodles

1 pound fine somen noodles (available at Asian markets)
2 tablespoons Oriental sesame oil
½ cup chopped fresh cilantro plus fresh sprigs for garnish
6 green onions, thinly sliced diagonally
½-1 cup chopped roasted peanuts for garnish

1) In a kettle of salted boiling water, boil the noodles for 3 minutes or until they are just tender.

2) Drain in a colander and rinse under cold water until noodles are cool.

3) In a large bowl, toss the noodles well with the oil, the chopped cilantro and green onions. The noodles can be prepared up to this point one day in advance and kept covered and chilled. Just before serving, toss the noodles with the peanut sauce to coat them well and garnish with cilantro sprigs and chopped peanuts. ✎

To keep salt flowing freely in the salt shaker, add a few grains of rice to absorb moisture. Remember to keep the salt in a warm, dry place.

This salsa is best made and refrigerated at least 6 hours before serving. It can be milder by omitting the peppers or as hot as you like with 3 or more jalapeños. You can also lavishly spoon it over a baked potato for a low-cal, satisfying meal.

FRESH TOMATO SALSA, GUACAMOLE and HOMEMADE TOSTADAS

Salsa
Makes 1 quart, serving 6 to 8

3 fresh jalapeño peppers, seeded and minced
8 very ripe medium tomatoes, chopped
2 medium Bermuda onions, diced
2 tablespoons olive oil
½ cup coarsely chopped cilantro leaves
½ cup coarsely chopped Italian parsley leaves
salt, freshly ground black pepper

1) Wearing rubber gloves, seed and chop jalapeño peppers.

2) Combine all ingredients in a mixing bowl. Season with salt and pepper. Refrigerate until ready to use.

Guacamole
Serves 6 to 8

Add 2 or 3 tablespoons of Fresh Tomato Salsa to 3 or 4 very ripe, unbruised, mashed avocados and you'll have the same fabulous guacamole I often serve.

Tostadas
Serves 6 to 8

12 fresh corn tortillas
4 cups corn oil
2 teaspoons salt

1) Cut the tortillas into 6 equal wedges.

2) In a heavy-bottomed pan, heat the oil to 375°F. You can tell if it's hot enough when you drop a tortilla wedge in the oil and it starts to sizzle.

3) Lightly fry the tortilla wedges in the oil until golden. Remove with tongs. You can do this in 2 or 3 batches, depending upon the size of your pan.

4) Put the chips into a paper bag and add the salt. Close tightly and toss. Serve warm or at room temperature. ✒

NACHOS
Nachos are simply tortilla chips covered with jack, cheddar or jalapeno cheese baked at 375°F until melted, then topped with almost anything your taste desires. Some popular condiments are refried beans, chopped onions, green onions, chilies, olives, sour cream, ground beef and sweet and hot peppers It's also delicious topped with guacamole, Fresh Tomato Salsa and the following Mango Salsa.

MANGO SALSA
Makes 2 cups

1 ripe mango
¼ cup finely diced red onion
1 teaspoon minced serrano chile, or more as
   desired
3½ tablespoons fresh lime juice
⅓ cup coarsely chopped cilantro
2 tablespoons coarsely chopped fresh basil
   (optional)
freshly ground black pepper
fresh cilantro for garnish

1) Remove the mango peel with a vegetable peeler. Using a thin, sharp knife, slice around the pit to remove the fruit. Cut into ¼-inch-thick strips and then cut crosswise into ¼-inch diced pieces.

2) Place the chopped mango in a medium bowl and add the onion, chile, lime juice, cilantro, basil and pepper to taste. Combine and adjust the seasonings to taste. Garnish with fresh cilantro leaves. ✒

My Decadent Dalliance

One of the best things about being a caterer is that so many jobs are celebrations. That was the case when I catered a party for Danny DeVito and Rhea Perlman. Long before Danny directed or starred in hit features like *Batman*, *War of the Roses*, *Twins*, *L.A. Confidential*, or *The Rainmaker*, Rhea was pregnant with their first child. Both of their careers were firecracker hot. She was enjoying tremendous reviews from *Cheers* and Danny's series, *Taxi*, was a blockbuster. All their years as struggling actors had paid off and they were ecstatic. They were living in a house they had recently purchased just north of Hollywood Boulevard, at the base of the Hollywood Hills. Although smaller than the home they now reside in, it was an absolutely charming house that dwarfed the compact duplex they had previously rented near Paramount Studios. It even had a dance studio for Rhea.

It was time to celebrate.

"Only the best" was the party *modus operandi* for this unpretentious couple. Driving down famed Sunset Boulevard following our meeting, "only the best" echoed in my mind as I pondered what precious delight I could serve at their party that would symbolize their huge success. That phrase stayed with me as my car turned onto Vine while my thoughts drifted up to Elizabeth Taylor's bedroom . . .

There she was introducing me to the most decadently delicious delicacy savored internationally by the rich and famous. At the time, Elizabeth was dating an Iranian diplomat who would shower her with pounds of the very finest Beluga caviar. Being the generous person that she is, Elizabeth invited me to partake in her private afternoon delight. Sensing my apprehension, she urged me to try these exquisite sapphires from the sea and I'm glad she did! As we spent the afternoon in her boudoir visiting, laughing and devouring spoonfuls of the most scrumptious thing I had ever tasted, I remember thinking to myself in between sips of Champagne that life just couldn't get any better!

So by the time I reached home I knew one item to definitely include at Danny and Rhea's party – Beluga caviar (the only type I recommend, and one of those items you just can't make). It was enjoyed by party guests including Tony Danza, Ted Danson, Henry Winkler, Shelley Long, Kelsey Grammer, John Ratzenberger, George Wendt, Melanie Mayron and many others.

Following the party was the perfunctory cleanup routine: the one thing hostesses hate and caterers dread. Because one of the challenges of catering is insuring that things are beautiful before, during and after, you have to be a laundry expert and kitchen chemist! In any event, I was prepared. For as we all know, anyone can drop anything at anytime. And Rhea, just like all of us who have fine carpeting, was concerned. So there I was, down on my knees, agonizingly inspecting her carpet, with my back aching and sciatica killing me, thinking there had to be something better in life. Just then a beam of light twinkled at me. It was gleaming off something in the kitchen right into my eyes. Intrigued, I got up to investigate, only to discover it was bouncing off the empty caviar tin. As a smile slowly washed over my face, my aches and pains vanished and I returned to the carpet, recalling better days in Elizabeth's bedroom. ✑

Anyone who hates caviar has not tasted Beluga. It is far superior to other varieties such as Smoked Salmon Caviar, American Black, Salmon Caviar or American Golden. For caviar is like Champagne: Just as the only real Champagne comes from the Champagne grape region in France, the only real caviar comes from the Caspian Sea. Russian royals eat it on buttered pumpernickel bread. Give it a try! Or, if you prefer, simple toast points are delicious with it. Present the caviar in its tin, top removed, in a bowl large enough to hold the caviar tin resting on crushed ice. (Never serve in silver – it will ruin the taste.) Place the bowl on a large platter and surround it with these condiments:

CAVIAR

separated and chopped hard-cooked egg whites and egg yolks
sour cream
chopped white onion
lemon wedges
toast points (white bread toasted, crust removed, cut in half diagonally) ✑

Pâté to this day still remains the classic appetizer. Despite the complexity of these two recipes, their elegance makes it well worth the effort. I have many friends who won't cook a recipe with more than three steps. What a loss! The way to approach a complex recipe is to read it two or three times, making sure you understand it. Provide yourself with a clear, clean working space. Gather all ingredients and measure them individually before you begin.

COUNTRY PÂTÉ
Serves 10

1 pound ground pork
½ pound ground veal
¾ pound ground rabbit
1 pound ground pork fat
1 small onion, minced
1 shallot, minced
3 garlic cloves, minced
½ tablespoon dried thyme
1 apple, peeled, cored and minced
½ tablespoon allspice
½ tablespoon salt
½ tablespoon freshly ground black pepper
½ cup brandy
2 eggs, lightly beaten
6 crushed juniper berries (available at health food stores)
½ pound of sliced bacon
6 pitted prunes, soaked in brandy
¼ pound lean rabbit meat, cut into strips
¼ cup whole hazelnuts
boiling water

1) Preheat oven to 325°F. In a large mixing bowl, combine all the ground meats, onion, shallot, garlic and apple.

2) In a separate bowl, combine the thyme, allspice, salt, pepper, brandy, eggs and juniper berries. Add the meat mixture and stir well.

3) Line a 6-cup terrine with ¾ of the bacon. Pack ½ of the mixture into the terrine and arrange the prunes down the center with the strips of rabbit and hazelnuts on both sides. Cover with the remaining mixture and top with remaining bacon.

4) Cover the pâté with foil and put into a baking pan that is 6 inches larger than the terrine. Fill the pan with boiling water and bake the pâté for 2 hours or until the internal temperature reaches 135°F. Remove from oven and cool.

5) Place some weights on top of the pâté to compress and eliminate excess water. (A gallon of milk works great.) Refrigerate up to 2 days.

6) Just before serving, gently run a knife around the edges to loosen and turn upside down to unmold. Serve at room temperature garnished with cornichons and accompanied by stone-ground mustard and a good corn rye bread. ✐

PÂTÉ with MUSHROOMS and PISTACHIOS
Serves 16 as an appetizer, 8 as a first course

8 large shallots
3 cloves of garlic
¾ pound boneless pork shoulder, cut into 2-inch cubes

¾ pound boneless veal shoulder, cut into 2-inch cubes
¾ pound bacon, cut into 2-inch pieces
2 tablespoons freshly ground black pepper
2 teaspoons dried thyme
1 teaspoon salt
½ teaspoon allspice
2 ounces assorted dried wild mushrooms, such as chanterelle, morel or shiitaki
1 cup Madeira wine
2 large eggs, beaten lightly
1 cup minced fresh parsley leaves
¾ cup shelled, natural pistachios
6 ounces smoked tongue

1) In a food processor, finely chop the shallots and garlic with the motor pulsing. Transfer to a large bowl.

2) In the same food processor, separately grind the pork, the veal and the bacon with the motor pulsing until the meat is the texture of ground chuck. Add to the bowl containing the shallot mixture. Add pepper, thyme, salt and allspice and combine well. Cover with plastic wrap and chill overnight.

The next day,

3) Preheat the oven to 375°F and butter a 2-quart terrine or a loaf pan.

4) Simmer the mushrooms in the Madeira for 5 minutes and let stand for 1 hour.

5) Drain the mushrooms, reserving the liquid,

and chop the mushrooms coarsely. Strain the liquid through a sieve lined with a moist paper towel. Add the liquid to the meat mixture.

6) Add the mushrooms, eggs, parsley, pistachios and tongue to the meat mixture and combine well.

7) Place a tablespoon of the meat mixture in a sauté pan and cook for a few minutes to taste for seasoning. Add more spices to taste.

8) Spread the mixture in the terrine and smooth the top. Cover with a double thickness of foil and bake in the middle of the oven until juices are no longer pink, about 1 ½ hours to 1 ¾ hours. Remove foil, cool on a rack for 30 minutes.

9) Cover surface of pâté with a double thickness of foil and weight it with 2 1-pound weights such as filled cans of beans, soup, etc. and chill overnight.

10) Pass a knife around the edge of the terrine and remove the pâté to a colorful serving plate. Garnish with sprigs of parsley and serve at room temperature with cornichons, crusty bread or pumpernickel and stone-ground mustard. ✐

Brandied **Gravlax**

This recipe is lighter than smoked lox because it has less salt and oil. I serve this a number of ways: At a formal sit-down, I slice it razor thin and present it on a salad plate drizzled with the mustard sauce, accompanied by pumpernickel points. For passed hors d' oeuvres, I serve it sliced razor thin in mounds atop cocktail-size pumpernickel or rye bread spread with the Mustard Dill Sauce garnished with a sprig of dill and a few capers. The morning after the party, I like to eat it with a bagel and cream cheese.

BRANDIED GRAVLAX with MUSTARD DILL SAUCE
Serves 10 to 12 as a first course

2 large bunches fresh dill
3½ or 4-pound section of fresh salmon
   preferably cut from the center of the fish
¼ cup kosher salt
¼ cup sugar
1 teaspoon coarsely ground white pepper
2 tablespoons brandy
capers for garnish

1) Cut off and discard any tough stems from the dill. Rinse the dill and pat dry.

2) Bone the salmon or have it boned. There should be 2 fillets of equal size and weight. Do not rinse the fish, but pat it dry with paper towels. Run your fingers along the fillet to feel for any bones and remove them with tweezers or needle-nose pliers.

3) Combine the salt, sugar and pepper. Rub the mixture into the pink flesh of the salmon. Sprinkle a few drops of brandy over the fillets.

4) Spread ⅓ of the dill over the bottom of a flat dish. Add 1 of the salmon pieces, skin side down. Cover this with another ⅓ of the dill. Add the remaining piece of salmon, placing it sandwich fashion over the dill, skin side up. Cover with the remaining dill and place a plate on top. Add a sizable weight and let stand in a very cool place or in the refrigerator for 48 hours. Turn the sandwich every 12 hours and marinate the salmon flesh with the accumulated juices, always covering with the plate and weighting it down.

5) Wipe the salmon clean with paper towels. Serve thinly sliced on the bias, with Mustard Dill Sauce. Garnish with capers and sprigs of fresh dill and capers.

Mustard Dill Sauce
Makes 1½ cups

½ cup Dijon-style, Dusseldorf or
   dark prepared mustard
2 teaspoons dry mustard
6 tablespoons sugar
½ cup white distilled vinegar
⅔ cup vegetable oil
½ cup chopped fresh dill
salt to taste

Combine the prepared mustard, the dry mustard and the sugar in a mixing bowl. Using a wire whisk, stir in the vinegar. Gradually add the oil, stirring rapidly with the whisk. Add the dill and the salt. Taste and correct the flavors by gradually adding more sugar, vinegar or salt. ✒

If the long list of ingredients for the other pâté recipes scared you — take heart: This one that I learned from Sandra Russo of Miami is fast, flavorful and always a hit.

SALMON WALNUT PÂTÉ

1 pound fresh cooked salmon, bones and skin
   removed,
or
1 16-ounce can of salmon, drained,
   bones and skin removed
1 8-ounce package cream cheese (not whipped)
½ teaspoon red horseradish
1 tablespoon lemon juice
1 or 2 tablespoons grated onion
¼ teaspoon Wright's Natural Hickory Seasoning
   Liquid Smoke
½ cup chopped walnuts
½ cup fresh chopped parsley
dash of salt

41

1) Flake the salmon and then mix together with everything except the nuts and parsley. Refrigerate covered for 1 hour.

2) Form into a ball or loaf.

3) In a separate flat dish, mix the parsley and nuts together, adding a dash of salt. Gently roll the ball or loaf onto the mixture, holding firm the shape you wish. Fill in any uncoated areas with the remaining mixture. Cover and refrigerate until ready to serve. I present this on glass decorated with grapefruit leaves and accompanied by crackers. ✒

CO-STARS!

c h a p t e r 3

The term "co-star" in film refers to an actor whose name is listed right next to or under that of the star. Chances are they are every bit as talented as the star, they just don't get top billing. In all cases, the co-stars always support the stars by complementing their characters and bringing out their best qualities.

With cuisine, the same is true of the term "side dish." This all important component of the meal makes the entrée look and taste even better. It provides an epicurean balance that otherwise would make the meal seem incomplete. What's turkey without stuffing, or steak without potatoes or chicken without dumplings or your favorite grain, pasta, vegetable or salad?

In many instances on screen, co-stars have come to stand on their own, obtaining "star" status. That is true of some recipes in this chapter – especially the risottos and salads. People enjoy the unique qualities of the individual offering and are satisfied with just that – and nothing more. Either way, these are the side dishes that are most frequently requested and I offer them to be served as side dishes, combined with other side dishes, or on their own. Another option that is currently in vogue is to take your guests "grazing," with an entire meal of side dishes. Consider serving six different salads, two or three to a plate. This will comprise a completely satisfying meal, plus it will offer your guests a variety of tastes. I like to combine my Honey-Kir Fresh Fruit Salad and the cold Classic California Pasta Salad with the Caesar Salad with my Homemade Parmesan Croutons on one plate. Then on the other, I serve Tarragon Turkey Salad, Caprese Salad and the refreshing, crisp Cucumber Salad with Dill. Grazing is fun and a unique party style that leaves a lasting memory.

I Wish I Had an Agent

Caterers and actors have two things in common: We want to do our best work possible, and we always hope the next job brings more recognition and money. What we don't have in common is an agent. An agent functions for an actor in numerous ways, but I think the most important thing they do is endeavor to see that their clients only accept a job that's befitting, that they get the best bucks and the best billing. That's why I wish I had one. Here's why.

My friend Rochell Linker Goodrich had a girlfriend whose brother was getting married. She had recommended me as the caterer and said to expect a call from a Los Angeles socialite and mother of the groom, Marjorie Volk. Several days later she called and we arranged to meet at her Santa Monica Mountains home. A stunning blond answered the door. It was Marjorie and she looked as if she had stepped right out of a page from *Vanity Fair*. Her contemporary home with its dramatic view of the city was the perfect setting for a wedding. Sleek and elegant with high ceilings and polished marble floors, the house was absent of any decorating "signs." What I mean is, most people like to decorate with things that reflect their personality, work and hobbies. Film producers have movie posters, actresses have photographs, hobbyists have collections displayed. This house just had stunning decor, and Marjorie was the focal point. She was

Raddicchio, Arugula & Frisee Salad

As a rule of thumb when making a salad, you can figure 2 lettuce leaves (romaine, red leaf, salad bowl, etc.) per person. This salad is the exception because of the small leaves, so be prepared to adjust the quantity of greens as you feel necessary. Tender leaves from the center of curly endive may be substituted for frisée.

RADICCHIO, ARUGULA and FRISÉE SALAD with ORANGES, WALNUTS and ROQUEFORT in WALNUT CHAMPAGNE VINAIGRETTE
Serves 6-8

16 radicchio leaves
8 frisée leaves
16 arugula leaves
6 tablespoons champagne vinegar
1 tablespoon Dijon-style mustard
1 garlic clove
½ cup walnut oil
2 tablespoons orange juice
salt and freshly cracked black pepper
3 navel oranges, peeled and sectioned
½ cup chopped walnuts
¼ pound crumbled Roquefort cheese

1) Wash and thoroughly dry the salad greens.

2) Break the radicchio, frisée and arugula into bite-size pieces. Chill covered with a moist paper towel.

3) In a blender or food processor, blend the vinegar and mustard and with the machine running, drop in the garlic and add the oil in a slow stream until blended. Add orange juice, salt and black pepper to taste.

4) Chill the dressing until ready to serve. Toss lightly being sure to underdress the salad.

5) Arrange the orange segments over the salad. Sprinkle with walnuts and Roquefort cheese. ✐

The following recipe calls for poaching a fresh turkey breast. It also works well with leftover roasted turkey breast. To reduce the fat content, select low-fat mayonnaise and nonfat sour cream. The dish makes an ideal meal accompanied by my Garden Salad, Honey-Kir Fresh Fruit Salad and a brioche.

TARRAGON TURKEY SALAD
Serves 4-6

8 cups chicken broth or water or a combination
1 small onion stuck with a clove
6-8 black peppercorns
2 bay leaves
2½- to 3-pound turkey breast,
6-8 cups broccoli florets cut with short stems
4 cups red wine vinegar
5 heaping tablespoons dried tarragon leaves
1 cup mayonnaise (regular or low-fat)
1 cup sour cream (regular or nonfat)
1 cup toasted pecans
salt and black pepper to taste
seedless grapes and red lettuce leaves for garnish

charming, very gracious and extremely comfortable to be with. In fact, I felt as if I knew her. Had we met before? There was this comforting familiarity about her – a friendliness uncommon for socialites who can sometimes be a bit standoffish.

Before I left, however, I realized I was wrong when I judged that the house had no visible signs. In the master bathroom, complementing the mandatory classic plumbing, was lighting more appropriate for open-heart surgery than washing one's face. And on the vanity were lotions, potions and perfumes to rival any Bloomingdale's cosmetic counter. Ah ha! This was a *professional* bathroom. A very definite sign!

Several days later, I called to thank Rochell for the referral and asked if I had met Marjorie before. Rochell explained I had, but not in person. Marjorie Volk was better known as Marjorie Lord, the marvelous mom opposite Danny Thomas in the hit TV series, *Make Room for Daddy*. Not only was she a former TV actress and soon-to-be mother of the groom, but she was also the mother of Rochell's friend, the talented actress Anne Archer, whose many credits include playing Michael Douglas's wife in *Fatal Attraction*.

No wonder I felt so comfortable with Marjorie. I knew her from television. And that explained that bathroom. All stars have them!

Soon thereafter, the wedding day arrived with the ceremony taking place on the large terrace overlooking Beverly Hills. I arranged the chairs in a semicircle where the bride and groom, surrounded by flowers, appeared to be floating over the city. After the service, the guests went inside while I set up tables for the sunset dinner on the terrace. It was an afternoon and evening of elegance and luxury, and Marjorie was profusely pleased with the event.

A few days later, when I was thinking that business just *couldn't* get any better, I received an urgent plea for help from a very talented caterer named Bruce Goldberg who needed my assistance at one of the biggest social events in Los Angeles. In the Hollywood catering world, everyone knows everyone, and I had known Bruce for years. It was hard to refuse a friend. Besides, it was the social event of the season, or as Bruce explained, if a bomb fell on the Music Center, there would be no socialites left in the city.

So, there I was at this mega affair at the Dorothy Chandler Pavilion lobby wearing my white linen jacket ready to work. As job duties were assigned, I was instantly embarrassed to realize that I had the dubious honor of serving Dorothy Chandler's favorite hors d'oeuvres: salted almonds upon a silver tray.

The hall was packed with socialites sporting their dazzling gems. More heads turned than in *The Exorcist*. In the midst of all this glitter, a beautifully groomed woman turned around, dropped her jaw and inquired what I was doing there. It was Marjorie, stunned to find her very own caterer serving nuts at someone else's party.

I realized by Marjorie's expression that

1) In a 4-quart kettle, bring the broth or water to a boil and add the onion, peppercorns, bay leaves and turkey breast. Reduce the heat to a medium simmer and poach the turkey breast for about 45 minutes or until cooked, turning it only once.

2) Remove kettle from the heat and allow the turkey to cool in the liquid. Remove turkey from the kettle. Strain the poaching liquid through a fine sieve and return to a boil. Then add the broccoli florets, blanching until still crisp, about 5 to 10 minutes. Remove broccoli from liquid, run under cold water to stop the cooking process and set aside.

3) Making sure you have good ventilation, simmer the vinegar and the tarragon in a saucepan until all the vinegar is reduced and you're left with only moist tarragon leaves. Be sure that no liquid remains or the dressing will be too tart. Be careful not to directly inhale the fumes from the evaporating vinegar, which can be overwhelming.

people do not want to see their caterer in a less than prestigious light. It diminishes one's perceived professional value. And so I made a vow never again to work the floor of any party other than my own. It was a long time before Marjorie thought of me for another occasion. But it was a lesson well learned. If I had only had an agent! ✍

4) Cut turkey into 1-inch cubes.

5) In a bowl, mix together 1 cup mayonnaise and 1 cup sour cream. Whisk in the moist tarragon leaves until well blended.

6) In a bowl large enough to hold the turkey, broccoli and half the pecans, dress the salad with the tarragon dressing (be careful not to overdress), salt and pepper. Garnish with remaining pecans and seedless grapes and serve on a red lettuce leaf. ✍

One afternoon I made this salad for Elizabeth. She enthusiastically said I should bottle the dressing and sell it. Well, I haven't sold it, but I will share it with you and hope it pleases your guests as much as it does Elizabeth. If egg safety is a problem in your area, use an egg substitute such as Egg Beaters as noted.

CAESAR SALAD and DRESSING with HOMEMADE PARMESAN CROUTONS
Serves 10

1 2-ounce can anchovies with oil
2 tablespoons fresh lemon juice
2 eggs★
4 dashes Worcestershire sauce
2 tablespoons Dijon-style mustard
2 cloves of garlic
1½ cups olive oil
1 cup freshly grated Parmesan cheese
freshly ground black pepper to taste
2 heads of romaine lettuce, outer leaves removed

★Or use one cup of Egg Beaters and increase lemon juice to 4 tablespoons total.

1) In a blender or food processor, blend the anchovies, eggs, lemon juice, Worcestershire sauce and the mustard. While the machine is running, drop in the garlic cloves 1 at a time.

2) Add the oil slowly while the machine is running, then add the cheese and the freshly ground black pepper.

3) Pour dressing over romaine lettuce and toss. Add croutons and toss again.

Parmesan Croutons

½ to ¾ cup sweet butter
1 tablespoon olive oil
3 cloves garlic, minced
1 loaf day-old French bread, cut into 1-inch cubes
1 teaspoon onion powder
¾ cup freshly grated Parmesan cheese
1 tablespoon paprika

1) Preheat oven to 400°F. In a heavy-bottomed sauté pan, heat the butter and oil, add garlic and sauté over medium heat being careful not to burn the garlic.

2) When the garlic turns transparent, pour it over the bread in a stream, tossing the pieces so they are evenly coated.

3) Place the bread pieces on a cookie sheet being careful not to crowd. Bake until golden brown, turning the croutons every couple of minutes to ensure even toasting.

4) Pour the croutons into a paper sack with the onion powder, grated cheese and paprika and toss well. Croutons will keep for several weeks in a tightly sealed jar. ✐

GARDEN SALAD with SHERRY VINAIGRETTE
Serves 6

1 shallot, minced
¼ bunch chives, minced
2 teaspoons Dijon-style mustard
6 tablespoons sherry vinegar
¼ cup olive oil
12 cups torn mixed lettuces such as romaine, red leaf, Boston and Bibb
salt and black pepper to taste

1) In a bowl, whisk together shallot, chives, mustard and vinegar, salt and black pepper until well combined.

2) Add the oil in a slow stream while whisking.

3) In a large bowl, toss lettuces with vinaigrette until coated well and serve.

Vinaigrette may be made 1 day ahead and chilled. Whisk before using. ✐

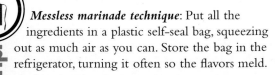

Messless marinade technique: Put all the ingredients in a plastic self-seal bag, squeezing out as much air as you can. Store the bag in the refrigerator, turning it often so the flavors meld.

Nick's Tip!

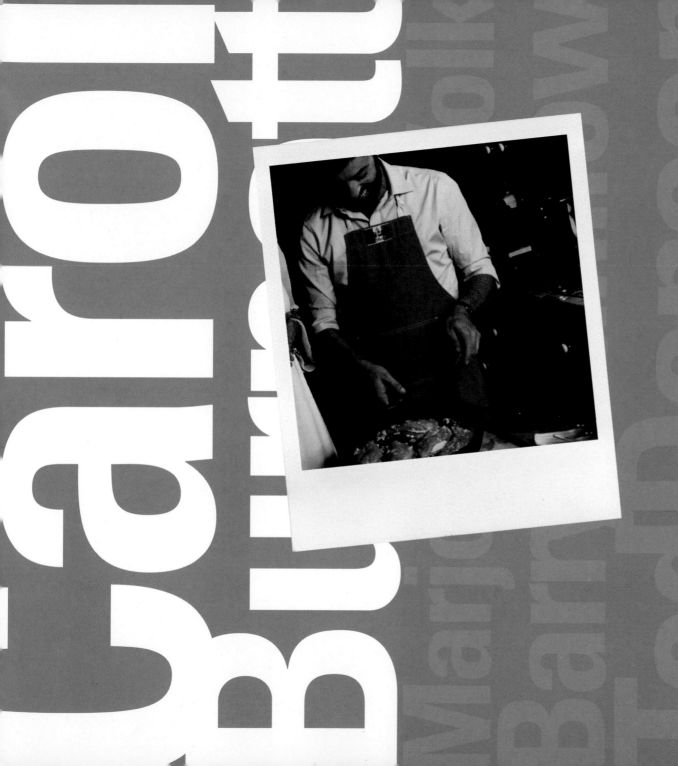

True Confessions

You can't help being simply amazed at the things people will confess when you listen to the radio or watch television talk shows. It's almost as if the moment the mike turns on or the cameras roll, they all open up their closet and empty everything out. Confessions that would make your socks roll up and down. Insults that are so cruel they could peel the paint off walls. Women who cut off their sister's hair while they sleep; mothers who steal their daughters' boyfriends; men who dress up like Cleopatra. What is it about the media that makes people want to tell all – to millions of strangers? Why do people have this need to confess?

I don't know if I have the answer. I'm a pretty private person. But I did surprise myself by making a personal confession to actress-comedienne, Carol Burnett the very first time I met her.

Carol and Elizabeth Taylor had filmed the television movie *Best Friends* and had become just that. Sometime later, Elizabeth and Richard Burton starred in the play *Private Lives* on Broadway and in Los Angeles. At the close of the L.A. production, Elizabeth threw a cast and crew party and invited Carol.

It was an outdoor barbecue by the pool at Elizabeth's Bel-Air home, and as always I was intrigued by which guests (who shall remain nameless) came fashionably late. Now some things you just can't be late for – especially a party hosted by Elizabeth Taylor! Anyway, I

*I find it amusing that I am so fond of this "nothing"
food that is a fungus without calories or fat — it's like
eating air that tastes great. Nevertheless, there's a trick
to selecting fresh mushrooms. Turn the mushrooms
upside down and check to see that the fibers are
connected to the stem. Make sure that you rub the
mushrooms clean with a moist cloth and don't wash
them, as they'll absorb water.*

MUSHROOM and CHIVE SALAD
Serves 6

1 pound mushrooms, stems discarded and the
   caps sliced medium fine
2 teaspoons fresh lemon juice
½ bunch chives chopped into ⅛" pieces
6 stalks celery, thinly sliced
2 tablespoons finely chopped fresh mint leaves
2 tablespoons finely chopped fresh cilantro
4 tablespoons extra-virgin olive oil
2 tablespoons white wine vinegar
½ teaspoon sugar
salt and pepper
red leaf lettuce for lining the platter

1) In a bowl, toss the mushrooms with the lemon
juice, chives and celery.

2) In another bowl, whisk together the mint,
cilantro, oil, vinegar, sugar, salt and pepper to taste.

3) Toss the mushroom mixture well with the
vinaigrette.

4) Wash and dry the red leaf lettuce and line a
large platter. Top with mushroom salad and serve. ✓

Everyone knows how to pick out a delicious strawberry: The obvious test is a rich, red color and sweet smell. Do not wash them if they will be stored, because strawberries are best when washed just before use.

HONEY-KIR FRESH FRUIT SALAD
Serves 8

⅓ cup honey
⅓ cup kir
1 tablespoon fresh lemon juice
2 pink grapefruit
2 navel oranges
1 pint strawberries, hulled and sliced
1 cup halved seedless grapes
3 kiwi peeled and cut into eighths

1) In a large bowl, whisk together the honey, kir and lemon juice. With a sharp knife, cut away the peel and the pith from the grapefruit and oranges. Working over the bowl, cut sections free from the membranes, letting the sections drop into the bowl and squeezing the membranes for juice.

2) Add the strawberries, grapes and kiwi and toss gently. Chill covered at least 1 hour or up to 3 hours.

served lots of grilled foods including burgers and ribs. And because Elizabeth had alerted me that Carol is a vegetarian, I made sure there was a bountiful offering of Caesar, potato, pasta and Caprese Salads.

I was looking forward to meeting Carol because I had so much to thank her for. You're probably thinking I was grateful for all those big laughs she provided me over the years on her many TV shows. I first started watching her on *The Garry Moore Show* and continued to enjoy her many comedy series. But Carol had given me something more important than laughs: She had given me a special kind of hope.

My son was majoring in hooky at Hollywood High (the very same school from which Carol had graduated.) When I finally realized he had a substance abuse problem, I searched for a program that would help.

If you've ever had a child who experiences such difficulties, you know all about guilt. In spite of the fact that his mother and I had a good relationship after our divorce, I couldn't stop blaming myself.

Carol Burnett was a parent with a similar situation. Like me, she was determined to help her child overcome a problem. She had located a twelve-step program that originated in Texas called the Palmer Drug Abuse Program, (PDAP for short) and helped bring it to L.A. To me, all substance abuse is the same. I don't care whether it's alcohol or drugs. You can't recover unless you stop using

the substance completely. The twelve steps are designed to help you do just that. What makes this program different is that it involves the parents. Since I couldn't ignore the fact that I was part of the problem, I was willing to be part of the solution.

So I felt this gratitude and kinship toward her. I looked forward to the moment when I knew Elizabeth would introduce us. As I often do, I had brought my son to help. While he had met his fair share of celebrities, like me, he felt a tie to Carol, too.

Sure enough, Elizabeth steered Carol our way and introduced us. Before she could finish complimenting my Caprese, the Grippo floodgates opened as a tidal wave of thanks engulfed Carol's humble shores. It was El Niño season that afternoon in Bel-Air and Carol Burnett got drenched. It couldn't have been more intense! In fact, it was like a water balloon contest between my son and me to see who could soak Carol with the most gratitude. Now mind you, absolutely no one was paying any attention to our conversation; no audience of millions listening. Just one very important person – Carol Burnett.

I had to leave early. Normally, clients would have a fit if their caterer did this (and they would be perfectly justified!), but Elizabeth, who has shared so much with me over the years, understood completely. Because of all places, I was off to a PDAP meeting. Some things you just can't be late for.

This easy, elegant salad will be all the more delicious if you are exceedingly careful when purchasing the ingredients. Not just any mozzarella cheese or tomato will do! Buffalo mozzarella, imported from Italy, is the very best choice and it's available at specialty food stores. Well worth the search! Vine-ripened tomartoes, now available at fine supermarkets (or preferably from your own yard) have the richest flavor. The superior taste of these two essential ingredients is guaranteed to heighten your enjoyment of this simple salad.

CAPRESE SALAD
Serves 2 as an appetizer or 1 for lunch

1 large, very ripe beefsteak tomato (preferably
    vine-ripened)
6 fresh basil leaves
1 fresh mozzarella ball (about the size of a golf
    ball) in water
5 tablespoons extra-virgin olive oil
4 tablespoons of the water from the mozzarella
    package
salt and fresh ground black pepper to taste
minced clove of garlic (optional)

1) Core the tomato and cut into ¼-inch slices.

2) Top each piece with a couple of basil leaves and a slice of mozzarella.

3) Whisk together the oil, water, salt and pepper and garlic and drizzle the mixture over the tomatoes.

4) Serve lightly chilled or at room temperature with crusty French bread. ✓

This salad is a natural mate with Poached Salmon or Brandied Gravlax. It also is a delicious accompaniment to many of the recipes in this book. Its mild flavor will enhance almost any breakfast, lunch or dinner buffet. I especially like serving it wth the Grilled Swordfish with Basil Butter, Fillet of Fresh Tuna with Pine Nuts and Shallot Sauce, as well as the Moussaka. What's best is that it can be made three hours prior to eating, leaving you time to prepare other dishes. P.S. Fresh dill is a must!

CUCUMBER SALAD with DILL
Serves 6-8

3 large cucumbers peeled, halved lengthwise
    and seeded
¾ cup chopped fresh dill
rind from 1 orange, grated
1 cup red wine vinegar
½ cup olive oil
¼ cup sugar

1) Cut the cucumber halves into crescents. Put them in a bowl with the dill and orange rind and toss.

2) Whisk together the vinegar, the oil and the sugar and pour over the salad. Refrigerate for 3 hours. Toss before serving. ✓

This is a good basic recipe that you can build upon. Just put a little pasta on a plate and add what you think might work. Try green pepper, petite green peas, green onions, petite white corn, green beans or sun-dried tomatoes. Experiment! For a lighter version, omit the olives and reduce oil to 1/4 cup.

CLASSIC CALIFORNIA PASTA SALAD
Serves 4 as a starter and 8 as a side dish

½ pound fusilli pasta
½ pound assorted pasta, such as penne, or bow-tie
½ cup olive oil
½ cup freshly grated Parmesan cheese
1 tablespoon minced garlic
1 teaspoon crushed red pepper flakes, or to taste
½ cup sautéed peas or broccoli
fresh ground pepper to taste
⅛ pound prosciutto
3 tablespoons chopped fresh basil
½ cup Greek olives, pitted and cut in half
¼ cup minced fresh parsley

1) Cook pastas separately according to package directions.

2) In a bowl large enough to hold all the ingredients, combine pastas, ¼ cup olive oil and cheese.

3) Sauté garlic in a saucepan with ¼ cup olive oil and crushed red pepper flakes until the garlic is opaque. Add your choice of vegetables and sauté until soft.

4) Add the sautéed vegetables to the pasta. Add fresh ground pepper to taste, prosciutto, basil and olives. Garnish with minced parsley and serve. ✓

My First Lady

One summer Elizabeth was renting a house in Malibu. Perched atop a humongous cliff overlooking Point Dume, it was a breathtaking home inside and out, with a marvelous expansive deck from which, on a clear day (no, I'm not going to say "you can see forever"), Catalina Island seemed just an arm's reach away. At the base of the cliff was the beachfront guest house. It was an exquisite property that just cried out for a festive barbecue. Elizabeth heard the plea and asked me to help her throw one in July. Delighted to oblige, I went over to check out the kitchen and serving opportunities.

Now it's been my experience with beach cliff homes that there seem to be two means of going from house to shore. One route is via stairs that descend straight down, evoking the same emotions that are stirred when you peer down from the top of the Empire State Building. Or, as it was in this case, a steep path about two blocks long that zigzagged its way down from house to beach. It was formidable for even the fittest, and was a hellish serpentine trek especially if one had to carry food, tables, umbrellas and all of the perfunctory paraphernalia for a successful party.

Elizabeth, who is an extremely creative hostess, felt that a beach barbecue wasn't a *beach* barbecue unless guests could tickle their toes in the sand. So we decided to start with

Greek Salad

Traditionally, lettuce was used only as a bed or a garnish for salad. Today, however, most people include lettuce as a major part of the salad. When it comes to Greek Salad, I am a traditionalist, preferring to emphasize the other ingredients that may also include sliced radishes, capers, green onions, watercress, chicory or fresh mint.

GREEK SALAD
Serves 6

crisp lettuce leaves
4 chilled beefsteak tomatoes
2 cucumbers, peeled, seeded and thickly sliced
1 medium red onion
   cut into eighths and separated
⅛ cup extra virgin olive oil
½ teaspoon dried oregano, crumbled
juice of ½ lemon
salt and freshly ground pepper to taste
½ to 1 cup feta cheese, crumbled
1 cup Greek Kalamata olives

1) Wash, dry and tear the lettuce into bite-size pieces. Arrange the lettuce in the center of a large platter.

2) Cover lettuce with tomatoes, cucumbers and onion.

3) Drizzle the olive oil over the salad, then sprinkle the oregano, salt and pepper and lemon juice. Top with crumbled feta cheese and olives and serve. ✓

appetizers at the shore followed by entrees on the main house deck. A golf cart was handy should anyone find the path foreboding.

Elizabeth's fifty guests included First Lady Nancy Reagan and her friend Marje Everett who both graciously declined an offer for a ride down the cliff. They favored the exercise and I watched with admiration as they ambitiously hoofed it down to the beach. The anonymous attendees were three secret service agents guarding the First Lady.

No sooner had I said "Come and get it" than a swarm of paparazzi buzzed overhead in planes. Evidently, and all too frequently, very unfortunately, photographers get wind of these kinds of celebrity gatherings. They're more loathsome than locusts (at least you can legally spray the bugs). The world knows how hard it is to call off photographers. But on this day that's literally what happened. One of the secret service agents got out his portable phone and within seconds it was bon voyage to the picture pirates. (Where was this man when we needed him at Elizabeth's wedding?)

Although I've cooked for many well-known people, this was my first experience with a First Lady and I was curious to see what foods she'd favor. I was also excited for another reason. Like all good sons, I knew it would thrill my mother no end to be able to say the First Lady sampled her Nicky's work. Now, all mothers get pleasure from bragging about their children, but I believe her boasting achieved a more important result. Because my mother has defied all odds and battled multiple sclerosis for more than forty years, I am convinced the vicarious pleasures I have provided her have helped her fight the illness. And so I was hoping to arm her subconscious with new ammunition.

Two observations I shared with Mom: Nancy Reagan's svelte figure is no accident. This lady keeps in shape (or otherwise it would have been impossible to manage that menacing slope to the beach). Plus, she's a light eater. With choices of ribs, burgers, buns, fried chicken, potato, Greek and Caesar salads, chili, baked beans, and strawberry shortcake, the only thing I saw her eat was a hot dog! The one thing I didn't make! But as I told Mom, I *did* prepare it. And I grilled it beautifully, I might add. ✓

This is an item I wouldn't think of making when delicious ones are available from Nate-N-Al in Beverly Hills. If you're in the neighborhood and in the mood for a "dog," stop by at 414 North Beverly Drive. Otherwise, take heart — they ship! Taste for yourself by calling 310-274-0101 to place an order.

HAUTE DOGS
Serves 1

1 hot dog
1 hot dog bun
condiments

To get a good-looking dog with traditional charred lines, allow the grill to get very hot before placing the hot dog on the grates. If you're doing a kids' party and want a fancy curly hot dog, before grilling cut a cross that's 1 ½ inches deep on each end of the dog. Serve with short rolls (or long dogs!) to allow the curls to show.

Once you've got a top-quality dog, the next most important part of this dish is an excellent roll. I prefer a sesame seed bakery roll garnished with the works: mustard, sweet relish, chopped onions, tomato wedge, pickle spear. When I was a kid, I'd eat them covered with French fries. ✓

57

When making this recipe, I prefer to use beer instead of bean water because it adds a special dimension. Baked beans take time to prepare. In the event your barbecue is spontaneous (I can admit to one or two), you can still serve great baked beans in a pinch by opening a can of baked vegetarian beans (or pork and beans) making sure to doctor with additional brown sugar, Worcestershire sauce and regular mustard.

BEER-BAKED BEANS
Serves 6

1½ cups dried red beans
¼ cup chopped onion
2 tablespoons (or more) dark molasses
3 tablespoons ketchup
1 tablespoon dry mustard
1 teaspoon salt
½ cup beer
½ teaspoon vinegar
1 tablespoon Worcestershire sauce
¼ pound sliced salt pork
well-seasoned chicken stock

1) Soak the beans covered in water overnight.

2) In an ovenproof kettle, bring the beans to a boil and simmer slowly for 30 minutes or until tender.

3) Preheat oven to 250°F. Drain the beans. Add the onion, molasses, ketchup, mustard, salt, ½ cup beer, vinegar and Worcestershire sauce.

4) Stir in the sliced salt pork and bake covered 6 to 9 hours. If the beans become dry, stir and add seasoned stock. During the last hour of cooking, uncover the beans. ✎

Baked Herbed Tomatoes are among those foods you wouldn't touch as a kid, but which can be quite a lovely discovery as an adult. I especially like serving the dish with a rich meal because the tomato adds a light refreshing dimension – not to mention the beautiful color. This recipe can also be prepared topped with buttered breadcrumbs.

BAKED HERBED TOMATO HALVES
Serves 6

6 ripe but firm tomatoes, cored and halved
¼ cup minced shallots
⅛ cup olive oil
2 garlic cloves, minced
¼ cup minced fresh parsley leaves
3 tablespoons freshly grated Parmesan cheese
½ teaspoon dried thyme, crumbled
3 tablespoons minced, fresh basil leaves
salt and freshly ground black pepper to taste

1) Preheat the oven to 375°F.

2) Gently squeeze the seeds and juice from the tomato halves. Arrange the halves in an oiled gratin dish.

3) In a bowl, combine the remaining ingredients and divide among the tomato halves. Drizzle remaining oil over tomatoes. (The tomatoes can be made up to 2 hours ahead to this point and kept refrigerated, covered.)

4) Bake the tomatoes uncovered in the middle of the oven for 20 minutes or until sizzling and the cheese is lightly golden. ✎

This is my basic potato salad. When I feel adventurous I add any number of ingredients including chopped dill or sweet pickles, capers, black or green pitted olives, cucumbers and Spanish onion. To reduce the fat I substitute low-fat mayonnaise and nonfat sour cream.

OLD-FASHIONED POTATO SALAD
Serves 8-10

3 pounds small new red potatoes
2 cups chicken broth
6 stalks celery
6 green onions, white parts only
6 hard-cooked eggs
2 teaspoons white horseradish
1 cup mayonnaise (regular or low-fat)
1 cup sour cream (regular or nonfat)
¼ teaspoon cayenne pepper, or to taste
salt and pepper to taste
chopped watercress
paprika

1) Cook the potatoes (skins on) in boiling salted water until tender. Slice the potatoes and place in a mixing bowl with the chicken broth and marinate covered for 2 hours.

2) Drain the potatoes. Coarsely chop the celery, green onions and 4 of the eggs. Add to the drained potatoes. Stir in the horseradish, mayonnaise and sour cream. Season with cayenne, salt and pepper and refrigerate for 1 hour before serving.

3) Arrange on a serving platter or in a bowl and garnish with 2 sliced hard-cooked eggs and chopped watercress. Dust with paprika. ✎

I Wish I Had a Publicist

It was a hot summer afternoon when he phoned. I hadn't begun to think about my fall parties. But that's just what Barry Manilow wanted. Booked for a lengthy tour through the holidays, Barry didn't want to miss celebrating his Thanksgiving meal at home. He wanted it early, and Elizabeth had given him my number. Why not!

Although we had never met, I had seen Barry perform early in his career as Bette Midler's piano accompanist. Like Bette, Barry's career had gone straight to the top. And thanks to radio airplay, TV and newspaper stories, I'd vicariously shared his ride. From his famous jingles including "You Deserve a Break Today" for McDonalds, to such now classic hits as "Mandy," "Even Now," "Looks Like We Made It," "Weekend in New England," "I Write the Songs," "Can't Smile Without You," "I Made It Through the Rain," his accomplishments are monumental. I love ballads, and Barry is a master at them. So, you can imagine how excited I was by the prospect of cooking for him. It was a thrill.

I wasn't sure what to expect as I drove to his house – it's always interesting to see the type of environment successful people choose. Barry's home made quite a statement.

It began with grounds that could accommodate a housing development. A meandering driveway led me to his house, just a stone's throw from the

At my house I always serve this traditional Thanksgiving dish garnished with available autumn leaves. One of the best things about living in Southern California is that I can always dash out into the yard and snip something colorful to use with the presentation.

SWEET POTATOES in ORANGE SKINS
Serves 6

4 pounds sweet potatoes
6 small unblemished navel oranges
2 eggs
1 tablespoon grated orange peel
¼ cup orange juice
2 tablespoons butter
salt to taste
½ teaspoon freshly grated nutmeg

1) Fill a large kettle with salted water and cook the potatoes covered for 30 to 40 minutes or until tender.

2) While the potatoes are cooking, cut the tops of the navel oranges with a small serrated knife, hollowing out the flesh; reserve for another use.

3) Drain, cool, peel and quarter the potatoes. Return them to the pot. Add the eggs, orange peel, orange juice and butter.

4) Mash and whip until smooth, adding the salt and nutmeg.

5) Heat the mixture and with a pastry bag fitted with a star tip, pipe the potato mixture into the hollowed orange skins. Serve on a platter garnished with autumn leaves. ✎

These pureed carrots are great alone but are a real showstopper when served piped into steamed lime-green summer squash. I hollow out the center of the squash, removing some flesh, and pipe in the pureed carrots. Just before serving I reheat in the oven. This works well on a buffet or when served family-style.

PUREED CARROTS in LIME-GREEN SQUASH
Serves 6

6 medium-size green summer squash
1 pound of carrots
1 egg
1 teaspoon grated orange peel
2 tablespoons unsalted butter
1 teaspoon salt
¼ teaspoon freshly grated nutmeg

1) Steam squash until tender but not mushy. Hollow out the centers of the squash.

2) Peel carrots, quarter and cook covered in salted water until tender, about for 20 to 30 minutes.

3) Drain and return to the pot. Add the egg, orange peel and butter. Mash and whip with a hand blender. Add salt and nutmeg.

4) Place the carrot mixture in a pastry bag with a star tip and fill the hollowed-out squash.

5) Heat in a 350°F. oven until warm. ✎

Bel-Air Hotel. I was pleasantly surprised when Barry answered the door, introduced himself and proceeded to give me a tour of his home while explaining what he had in mind for dinner. I couldn't help but admire the classic fifties-style habitat of uncluttered lines and lots of white, marble and glass. Very elegant.

Built on the side of a hill, Barry's house had an addition constructed that I could live in! Upstairs were lounge chairs, pinball machines, a bar – just a great fun room. Downstairs was a theater where Barry composed. Big windows supplied beautiful natural light until the push of a button closed the shades to darken the room for screening films. Decorating the walls were gold and platinum records, signifying easily a zillion dollars in record sales.

It was easy to tell that music, not food, was the big love of his life because the kitchen seemed basically untouched since the time the house was constructed. It had a built-in stove and an island typical of that time period. I also noticed he had an eclectic collection of serving pieces that obviously had sentimental value.

We decided on a traditional Thanksgiving dinner with all the trimmings, including Sweet Potatoes in Orange Skins. The intimate dinner took place shortly after Labor Day. I remember that Suzanne Somers and husband Alan Hamel were among others who enjoyed the feast served on Barry's own white bone china.

From that day forward, I did many

parties for Barry, including a birthday barbecue buffet on the lawn. But something I *didn't* do taught me a lesson I shall now share.

Now, as you probably know, schmoozing, or kibitzing or chatting – whatever you want to call it – is extremely important. Every good salesperson does it before sealing the deal. It's that warm-up time when pleasantries and subtle, key information are exchanged. Naturally, with Barry, we all know about his activities because a publicist has made sure he's written about. And we hear him on the radio, see him on TV and in concert. So someone like Barry doesn't need to schmooze with me. He knows I know about him. But for Barry to know what I'm doing, the schmooze is vitally important. How else could he know that I did the Citicorp opening party for five thousand people, the wedding for Robert Mitchum's granddaughter, the dinner for Coca-Cola or the wrap party for *E.T.*? The truth is, he couldn't and didn't.

And I naively assumed he did.

In the fall of 1990, I was tentatively booked to do a party for Barry following his New Year's Eve concert. But by December, I had heard nothing further. When I called to find out what was up, I was informed additional catering bids were being solicited.

Now believe me when I tell you that caterers are possessive of their clients. That's putting it mildly. We also make certain assumptions: like after doing a half-dozen parties for a client, a bid is not

CLASSIC MASHED POTATOES and GRAVY
Serves 8

4½ pounds russet (baking) potatoes
½ cup (1 stick) unsalted butter, softened
1 egg, room temperature
½ cup (about) whole milk, warmed
salt and white pepper to taste
Gravy pg. 77

1) Peel and quarter the potatoes and put into a kettle and cover with cold water by 2 inches. Bring to a boil and simmer 30 minutes or until the potatoes are very tender. Drain the potatoes.

2) With a potato masher, mash the potatoes and add the butter, the egg and the milk, a little at a time, to reach the desired consistency. Season with salt and pepper. ✓

CREAMED ONIONS
Serves 6

20 small, unpeeled white onions, about 1½ to 2 pounds
1 cup Béchamel Sauce pg. 96
dash of cloves
¼ teaspoon paprika
2 tablespoons sherry
minced celery
¼ cup chopped parsley

1) In a covered pan, steam the onions on a rack over (not in) boiling water until tender, approximately 20 to 30 minutes.

2) Peel the onions and heat with 1 cup Béchamel Sauce for l minute, then add cloves, paprika, sherry and celery. Garnish with parsley and serve. ✓

CREAMED SPINACH
Serves 3

1 clove garlic
1½ to 2 tablespoons butter
1 tablespoon white onion, finely chopped
1 tablespoon flour
½ cup cream, warmed
1 teaspoon sugar
freshly grated nutmeg or rind from ½ lemon
salt and black pepper to taste
2 cups boiled spinach, finely chopped
hard-cooked eggs for garnish

1) In a heavy-bottomed skillet, rub the clove of garlic lightly, then add the butter and onion and cook until the onion is golden.

2) Add the flour and stir until blended. Slowly add the warmed cream and sugar, stirring until sauce is smooth.

3) Add the spinach and cook, stirring for 3 minutes. Season with salt and freshly ground pepper and freshly grated nutmeg or lemon rind. Garnish with slices of hard-cooked eggs. ✓

61

Potatoes Gratin

necessary but a proposal is more appropriate. It would be like Barry's record company asking him to do a demo tape, or a movie studio asking Jack Nicholson to do a screen test. But I swallowed my pride and rushed in a formal bid.

The next day, I withdrew it. I felt *very* uncomfortable with the whole situation. One of Barry's associates told me they weren't aware that I could pull off such a large event. And therein was my problem. I was so busy with catering that I had overlooked an important business ingredient: publicity. I just *assumed* he knew about the western-style bar mitzvahs, the Fellini-style Halloween parties, the political fund-raisers. I knew what I had done. I thought Barry did too.

Wrong! The truth is, he couldn't know. Because I didn't tell him. Never one to brag, I would be uncomfortable recounting my accomplishments. I would rather clean ovens than name-drop a party at another client's affair. Obviously, I would have to put a shine on my accomplishments. This prompted me to start my newsletter, which I continue to this day (one of the best things I ever did), for which I will always thank Barry.

Anyway, the job went to a competitor while I did a spectacular New Year's Eve party for Cindy Williams. Since then I have catered again for Barry. And, to this day, he remains one of my favorite clients. I've never forgotten the important lessons from way back when: 1) Never assume people know your accomplishments, and 2) Remember to schmooze or else you lose. I wish I had a publicist. ✐

POTATO and YAM GRATIN with JARLSBERG
Serves 6-8

¾ pound small white boiling potatoes
¾ pound yams or sweet potatoes
1 clove garlic
1 cup coarsely grated Jarlsberg cheese
freshly grated nutmeg to taste
salt and freshly ground black pepper to taste
1½ tablespoons all-purpose flour
1 large egg
2 cups whole milk or cream, scalded
2 tablespoons cold, unsalted butter, cut in little bits

1) Preheat oven to 375°F. Peel and very thinly slice the potatoes, and using a food processor, or mandolin, which is a utensil for slicing and shredding.

2) Rub with garlic and lightly butter the inside of a 13 x 14-inch oval gratin dish (a 2-quart baking dish). Arrange the potatoes and the yams in a total of 4 alternating layers beginning with the white potatoes, sprinkling each layer with ⅓ cup of the Jarlsberg, some nutmeg, salt and pepper, and sprinkling the yam layers with flour.

3) In a bowl, whisk the egg, add the scalded milk in a stream, whisking, and pour evenly over the potato and yam mixture.

4) Sprinkle the remaining ⅓ cup Jarlsberg on top. Dot with butter and bake uncovered in the middle of the preheated oven for 45 minutes or until it is golden and bubbling and the potatoes are tender. ✐

BRAISED BROCCOLI in TOMATO CUPS
Serves 8

1½ large bunches of broccoli (about 3 pounds), separated into florets, with peeled, short stems
4 medium-size tomatoes
¾ cup olive oil
2 tablespoons minced fresh garlic
salt and freshly ground black pepper

1) Preheat the oven to 300°F. In a kettle of salted boiling water, add the broccoli and cook uncovered until crisp-tender, about 4 or 5 minutes. Drain and immediately plunge into ice water to stop the cooking process. Drain again and pat dry. (Broccoli can be prepared to this point several hours ahead.)

2) Core tomatoes and cut in half crosswise. Carefully remove pulp leaving ¼- to ½- inch shell. Invert halves on paper towels and set them aside to drain.

3) Generously butter a large baking dish. Heat the olive oil in a large skillet over medium-high heat until very hot. Remove from heat, stir in the garlic, add broccoli and toss gently to coat. Season with salt and pepper to taste.

4) Arrange broccoli stems side down in the tomato cups. Set the tomatoes in the lightly buttered baking dish. Bake until heated through, about 5 to 7 minutes. Arrange the tomato cups around a roast and serve. ✐

63

OLD-FASHIONED POTATOES GRATIN
Serves 4

2 pounds boiling potatoes
¾ cup chopped parsley
1 cup ricotta cheese
salt and freshly ground black pepper to taste
1 egg
1 cup heavy cream
unsalted butter for greasing the baking pan
¼ pound sharp white cheddar cheese
   (about 1 cup)
nutmeg to taste
minced chives or parsley for garnish

1) Preheat oven to 350°F. Peel the potatoes and
cut out any bad spots or eyes. Thinly slice them
and put into a pot of cold, salted water. Bring
the potatoes to a boil and parboil for 1 minute,
drain and rinse under cold running water. Pat
them dry.

2) Mix the parsley and the ricotta together and
add salt and pepper generously. Beat the egg and
add enough cream to make 1 cup of liquid.
Season with salt and pepper.

3) Lightly butter an oval gratin dish measuring
approximately 9x12 inches and arrange a layer of
potatoes overlapping in the dish. Dot with some
of the ricotta mixture. Sprinkle with ⅓ of the
cheddar cheese, season with a little fresh nutmeg
and repeat the process until all the ingredients
are used, ending up with potatoes on top.

4) Pour the egg and cream mixture evenly over
the potatoes.

5) Bake for 35 to 40 minutes until potatoes are
tender and the cheese is bubbly and brown. Wait
10 minutes before serving and garnish with
minced chives or parsley. ✓

BARRY MANILOW

Dear Nick —
Thanks for all of the first-
class dinners. You and your
company are the most reliable
and discreet caterers around.
Keep up the good work.
All my best. Barry Manilow

64

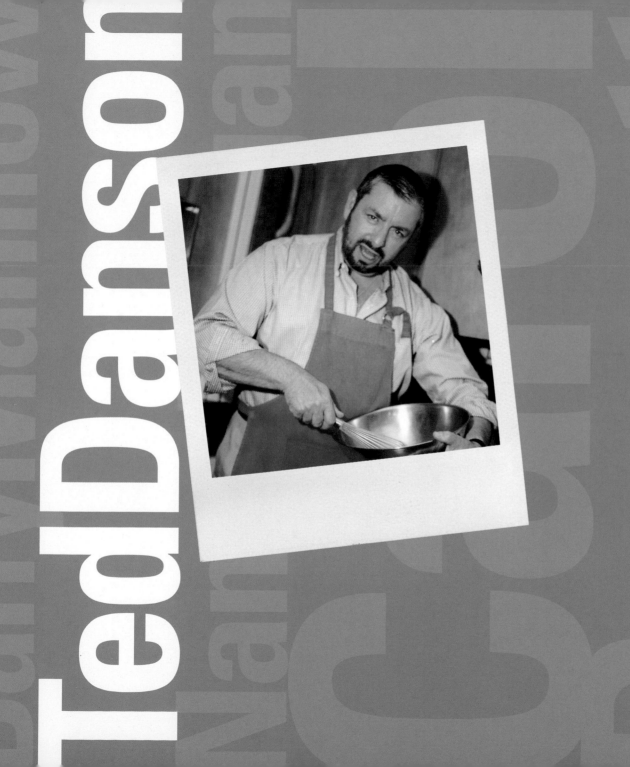

TedDanson

Real Men Wear Cologne

Never would I wear cologne. Ever. That is, never until I met Ted. I knew incredibly handsome Ted from Milton Katselas's acting class. There he was not just Ted Danson, fellow acting student. There he had another identity. Ted was "The Aramis Man," the epitome of tuxedoed masculinity in a TV commercial. Calm. Confident. Macho with a capital "M." God knows how many men wore cologne because of the way he emerged from that limousine holding that umbrella. Or how many women bought it hoping it would transform their beaus into Ted. Spying him in class, I wondered what kind of person he was. Was there an actor beneath that handsome exterior?

Ted was in Milton's class long enough for us to discover that not only could he act, but he also had fabulous comedic timing. I'll never forget the scene Ted did from *Taming of the Shrew*. Ted played Petruchio who was courting Kate the shrew, played by actress Nancy Stephens. Petruchio came to woo Kate because he wanted her dowry. The introductory scene, which is very popular in workshops, contains brilliant wordplay that's extremely cerebral. Well, they did a hysterical rendition of the lines, and they added a contemporary dimension by making it so physically slapstick that even Charlie Chaplin would have been envious. They wrestled, fought and dragged each other across the stage, managing to use every inch of space. It gave a glimpse of the physicality Ted uses in such films as *Body Heat*, where he tap-dances while waiting for William Hurt, and in *Three Men and a Baby*. He's quite an actor.

During class, Ted and I developed a friendship based on my adoration for the way he could turn a scene into a comedic uproar, while he enjoyed my laugh and my cooking.

Shortly after a few acting sessions, Ted was cast in a new TV show that would become a classic. It was simply called, *Cheers*. He dropped out of class, but we remained in contact through my catering services and through the friends he referred.

With the Christmas holidays fast approaching, Ted decided to throw a party to celebrate his birthday and the show's success. Being a genuinely thoughtful, warm fellow, Ted didn't want a stuffy, formal, sit-down evening. Instead, he preferred a friendly, inviting ambience. Ted suggested we line the driveway with luminarias, the way he did as a kid, and I made them by placing votive candles in the center of paper lunch bags filled with sand. It provided a wonderfully inviting welcome for arriving guests. Then we decided to serve the appetizers in the living room, and the buffet-style dinner on the dining room table.

More than eighty people came that night, including the entire cast of *Cheers*. This was Ted's first "big party" and there was a "nothing can stop us now" jubilance that comes when years of struggling, hoping and lots of hard work have paid off. Everyone was joyous and there was a wonderful camaraderie obvious between the stars Ted, Shelley Long, Danny DeVito and Rhea Perlman.

Just as actors get the jitters before going on stage, so do caterers. We want everything to be perfect . . . it absolutely has to be. On this night, I planned to make Spinach Risotto with Pine Nuts. But I had never made it for such a huge gathering. Prior to leaving for Ted's, I rechecked my list to ensure that I had everything. I knew I did, but for some reason something just didn't feel right. I made a quick run through my house. Lights on? No. Coffee pot? No. Just then I spotted an unopened bottle of cologne on my dresser.

Intrigued, I stared at it for some time. Mesmerized, I dabbed some on, picked up my umbrella and headed for the garage. After driving over the Cahuenga Pass, I arrived at Ted's, parked the car and emerged with inexplicable calm and confidence. I love cologne. ✑

This is an excellent side dish and one of the few ways I know to make risotto without standing by the pot stirring in the broth a cup at a time. As a savory substitute for potatoes, it goes well with grilled fish and roasted chicken.

SPINACH RISOTTO with PINE NUTS
Serves 6

2 pounds fresh spinach, washed and dried, stems removed
½ cup olive oil
2 medium onions, minced
1 garlic clove, minced
1 cup Arborio rice
2 tablespoons tomato sauce
2 bay leaves
salt and freshly ground pepper to taste
2 cups chicken broth
toasted pine nuts for garnish

1) Tear the spinach leaves into medium-size pieces. In a heavy-bottomed skillet, heat the olive oil and sauté the onions, garlic and rice until the onions are soft and golden. Stir in the tomato sauce.

2) Add the spinach, bay leaves, salt and pepper and mix well. Add the chicken broth. Cover and simmer on a very low flame for 20 minutes. Garnish with toasted pine nuts and serve on a platter. ✑

Nick's Tip!

Ever receive flowers that came with a packet of granules to add to the water? It's bleach! It prevents vase water from clouding up, and it reduces vase odor. You can accomplish the same thing by adding one tablespoon of bleach to each quart of water in your vase.

Spinach **Risotto** with Pine Nuts

This is a basic recipe. In northern Italy, this is a dietary staple much like pasta is in southern Italy. It's used as a base to add vegetables, meats, sausages, chicken, etc. The difference between this and regular rice is that this is a shorter grain and you must stay with it during the cooking process, stirring and adding broth until al dente. It should be smooth and runny as opposed to regular rice.

RISOTTO MILANESE
Serves 8

6 tablespoons unsalted butter
3 tablespoons finely chopped onion
1 clove garlic, minced
2 cups Arborio rice
1 tablespoon saffron
salt and freshly ground pepper
5 cups chicken broth
½ cup dry white wine
¾ cup freshly grated, imported Parmesan cheese
chopped parsley for garnish

1) Heat 4 tablespoons of the butter in a heavy-bottomed skillet. Add the onion, cook until translucent, then add the garlic and cook until it is wilted.

2) Add the rice, saffron, salt and pepper and stir to coat.

3) In a separate saucepan, heat the broth to simmer and hold.

4) To the rice, add the wine and stir until evaporated.

5) Add a cup of the broth to the rice mixture and stir until absorbed. Continue to add the remaining broth, cooking gently until the rice is cooked. This is not like regular rice, which is done when all liquid is absorbed. Risotto should have a slight bite and still be runny.

6) When all the broth has been absorbed to your liking (tasting along the way for the risotto to be *al dente* – not soft like regular rice), add the Parmesan cheese and the remaining 2 tablespoons of butter. Serve, garnished with chopped parsley. ✐

Over the years, I've conducted private cooking classes at the homes of many clients. I've held numerous classes in Carrie Fisher's house. It's a warm, casual environment where class members are taught cooking techniques and learn how to prepare the recipes they enjoy. A while back, Meryl Streep was in the group, and she wanted to learn how to make dumplings. Carrie thought she really meant pirogi (shades of Sophie's Choice?) which are Polish dumplings. Meryl wasn't exactly sure what kind she wanted to learn, so we put the request on hold until one night before class when Carrie called to alert me it would be Meryl's last session before leaving town for the summer. We had to make dumplings now! So, we did!
   Dumplings, an old-fashioned comfort food, are good only when served immediately from the pot. They don't lend themselves well to resting a long time in advance of serving. So plan on making dumplings the last thing you do before sitting down. This recipe works well with a variety of fresh herbs used either separately, or combined. My favorite is a mixture of dill and parsley.

HERBED DUMPLINGS
Makes 12

1½ cups all-purpose flour
½ cup yellow cornmeal
1 tablespoon double-acting baking powder
½ teaspoon salt
1 tablespoon minced fresh dill
1 tablespoon minced fresh parsley
a pinch of grated onion
1 cup plus 3 tablespoons half-and-half
2 or 3 cups of chicken stock

1) Sift together the flour, cornmeal, baking powder and salt. Stir in the grated onion and fresh herbs.

2) With a fork, stir in the half-and-half until the dough is just blended (or you'll end up with cement).

3) Bring the stock just to a boil. Dip a large soup spoon into the stock, then fill it with the batter and drop into stock. Repeat 12 times, making sure to first dip the spoon into the stock each time to prevent the batter from sticking to the spoon.

4) Cover and simmer 10 minutes. Dumplings are done when a toothpick inserted in the center comes out clean. Serve immediately. ✐

*Saffron is the diamond of spices. Very expensive –
but well worth the cost. I find that interesting
because it's also one of the first spices used by man,
not just for seasoning and coloring food, but for dying
fabrics. You'd think since it's been around so long, it
wouldn't be so expensive, but it is. In fact, you might
have to ask your store manager for this spice, which
is often kept under lock and key.*

SAFFRON RICE with CURRANTS AND PECANS
Serves 6

2 tablespoons vegetable oil
½ teaspoon cumin
1 cinnamon stick
1 bay leaf
1 cup finely chopped white onion
2 cups long-grain rice
2¼ cups chicken stock
⅓ cup currants
½ teaspoons salt
¼ teaspoon crumbled saffron threads
½ cup pecans cut into quarters and lightly
   toasted

fresh mint leaves for garnish

1) In a heavy saucepan, heat the oil over
moderate heat and cook the cumin, cinnamon
stick and bay leaf, stirring until the mixture is
fragrant, being careful not to burn.

2) Add the onion and cook until softened. Stir in
the rice and cook for 1 minute. Stir in the stock,
currants, salt and saffron, cover and bring to a

boil. Reduce the heat to very low and simmer
covered 20 minutes or until all the stock is
absorbed.

3) Let the rice rest for 5 minutes, discard the
cinnamon and bay leaf. Stir in the pecans,
garnish with fresh mint leaves and serve. ✓

STRATA CHEDDAR SOUFFLÉ
Serves 4 to 6

5 slices of a good white bread, crusts removed,
   slices lightly buttered on both sides
1 pound grated cheddar cheese
4 eggs, beaten
2 cups milk
½ teaspoon dry mustard
½ teaspoon salt
¼ teaspoon cayenne pepper

1) Preheat oven to 350°F. Butter a small soufflé
dish.

2) Make a layer of bread on the bottom of the
dish, add a layer of cheese. Continue layering in
this fashion ending with cheese on top.

3) Combine eggs, milk, dry mustard, salt and
pepper and pour evenly over cheese.

4) Bake for 1 hour and serve immediately.

This can be assembled the night before and
stored covered in the refrigerator. Cook 10
minutes longer if chilled. ✓

entrees

Ask people what their favorite film is and they'll mention the star. Ask what a favorite meal is and you'll hear about the main dish, not about an appetizer. You know just what I mean. Inviting someone over? It's for steak or pasta, not French fries or breadsticks. The entrée is the star of the meal all right. That's why it gets "top billing," meaning it's always mentioned first and foremost.

Choosing an entrée is like deciding what movie you want to see: ethnic, like Moussaka; western, such as Rodeo Drive Spareribs; or southern, such as Louisiana Baked Shrimp. The entrée says it all. And what you're in the mood for will dictate your choices. Presented on the next pages are a variety of entrées I've prepared for all kinds of moods and occasions. All dependable. All delicious.

You might want to consider a party of several entrees and create a "station party" like the menu I planned for the *E.T. Wrap Party* (see page 12). Guests get to select tastes from a number of choices that all work well together. The concept is that all of the dishes you select work interchangeably as entrees or side dishes. This way, your guests can decide what they want to eat and how they want to combine the tastes – it's an interactive menu. For example, at one station you can have Spaghetti alla Puttanesca, Louisiana Baked Shrimp at another, and Poached Salmon at yet another. The other plus of a station party is that all of the "stars" can be made well in advance, so you can join your guests as they move from station to station.

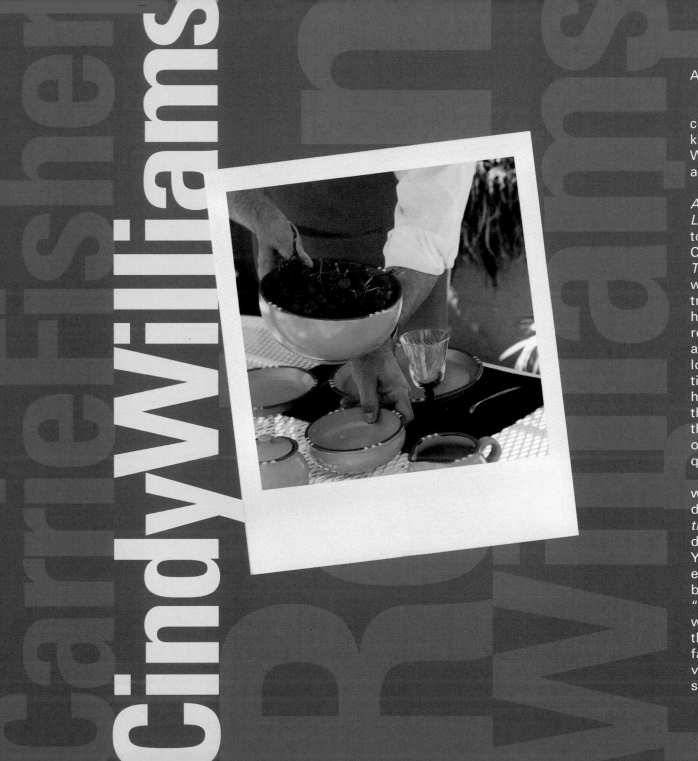

A Kick in the Pants

She was just eighteen and impishly cute. Never did I imagine I'd get such a kick out of fellow acting student Cindy Williams, or that she would make such an impression on me, *literally.*

Long before her first feature film, *American Graffiti,* or her hit TV series *Laverne & Shirley,* we did a play together while students at Los Angeles City College. It was Arthur Miller's *After The Fall.* I had a very small part in which I had to look like I was catching a train or a bus. New to acting, I had a hard time achieving the look of realizing I might miss my ride, kind of an anxiously hurried/terrified/startled look. I would enter the stage time and time again, never getting it right. Cindy had the solution: She *kicked* me onto the stage. It worked! From then on for the duration of the play, she would kick or push me on for my entrance. It was quite effective.

Cindy pushed me in other ways. She was the first person I dated after my divorce. Not that she pushed me into *that.* But it takes a while to get over a divorce, and dating Cindy was fun. Young and very energetic, she was effervescent, optimistic and a delight to be with. While I never viewed her as a "babe in the woods," I was surprised when she confessed to me years later that she thought I was so mature. In fact, as an eighteen-year-old, she viewed me (I was a very late twenty-something year old) as an *older man.*

This is a recipe I've prepared countless times for Elizabeth. Before you add the shortening, be sure the pan is very hot, that you use lots of spices, cook it very crispy and very well done if you want to experience it just the way Elizabeth does. While it's not low-calorie, I try to balance the meal with a light dessert. Squeeze lemon or lime juice on a summer melon garnished with mint for a low-cal finale.

SOUTHERN FRIED CHICKEN
Serves 4

1 quart buttermilk
1 large frying chicken, cut into pieces
flour for dredging
paprika
garlic powder to taste
cayenne pepper to taste
lemon pepper to taste
Mrs. Dash seasoning to taste★
2 cups vegetable shortening
2 cups (4 sticks) unsalted butter
★ Available at your local supermarket.

1) Place buttermilk and chicken in a large bowl, cover and soak overnight in the refrigerator.

2) Bring the chicken to room temperature. Mix the flour and all of the spices, in a large paper bag. Remove 1 piece of chicken at a time from the milk and shake in the flour mixture. Then remove from bag and let the piece rest on wax paper for at least ½ hour.

3) Heat a cast-iron skillet (large enough so the shortening and butter combination fills half of the pan). Heat the pan until it is too hot to touch, then add the shortening. Let shortening get hot and then add butter. When it is very hot, add the chicken pieces being careful not to crowd the pan. Frequently turn the chicken as it cooks. When it is crispy all over turn the heat down and continue cooking until the insides are cooked. Drain on paper towels and serve immediately or at room temperature. ✐

CHICKEN GUADALAJARA
Serves 6

1 3- to 4-pound chicken, boiled until the meat
    can be boned
    or 3 pounds chicken breasts, poached
1 24-ounce can of chopped tomatoes
1 large red onion chopped to medium coarseness
1 4-ounce can of green chilies, mild or hot,
    chopped
2 cloves garlic, minced
l cup vegetable oil
1 dozen corn tortillas
1 pound jack cheese, shredded
cilantro for garnish

1) Preheat oven to 350°F. Bone cooked chicken or shred cooked chicken breasts.

2) Combine tomatoes, onion, chilies and garlic in saucepan and simmer approximately 40 minutes.

3) Heat vegetable oil and fry tortillas a few at a time until golden brown and crisp; drain on paper towels. Break the fried tortillas into several large pieces.

4) Place a layer of broken tortillas on the bottom of a greased 9x13-inch casserole. Add the chicken pieces and cover with half the tomato mixture. Sprinkle with half of the cheese and repeat with another layer of tortillas, chicken and tomato mixture, ending with cheese on top.

5) Bake uncovered for 40 minutes or until the cheese is bubbly.

6) To serve, cut into squares and serve. Garnish with cilantro leaves. ✐

Chicken Piccata

If you get nervous cooking for company, this is a recipe you can count on. It's quick and easy and is the one dish most frequently requested by my clientele. In fact, Cindy insisted I serve it at her wedding to Bill Hudson.

CHICKEN PICCATA
Serves 4–8

4 whole chicken breasts, skinned, boned and
　halved
½ cup flour
1½ teaspoons salt
¼ teaspoon freshly ground pepper
¼ teaspoon paprika
¼ cup (½ stick) clarified butter
1 teaspoon olive oil
2 to 4 tablespoons dry Madeira or Marsala
3 tablespoons fresh lemon juice
lemon slices
3 to 4 tablespoons capers (optional)
½ cup minced fresh parsley, stems removed

1) Place chicken breasts between 2 sheets of waxed paper (or a quart-size plastic bag) and pound them until thin, about ¼ inch.

2) Combine the flour, salt, pepper and paprika in a bowl. Add the breasts and coat well; shake off excess.

3) Heat butter and olive oil in a large skillet until bubbling. Sauté the chicken breasts, a few at a time, 2 to 3 minutes on each side, being careful not to overcook. Drain on paper towels and keep warm.

When I asked her to go dancing once, she hesitated, thinking I meant ballroom style. And while I was old enough to appreciate opera, which I introduced to Cindy, ballroom dancing wasn't my thing. I like to move.

She pushed me in a supportive sense. In those days, there was no such thing as "joint custody." Visitation rights weren't all that flexible, and I only had my son on weekends. Cindy encouraged me to make the most of the precious moments I had with him. I still have fond memories of us all going to the L.A. Zoo together and having a family day.

4) Drain off all but 2 tablespoons of butter and oil. Stir Madeira into drippings, scraping bottom of skillet to loosen any browned bits. Add lemon juice and heat briefly.

5) Return chicken to skillet, interspersing with lemon slices and heat until sauce thickens. Add capers. To serve, place chicken and lemon slices on a platter and pour pan juices over the chicken. Garnish with capers and minced parsley.

Nick's Tip!

Cooking should be a pleasant experience – just like on those cooking shows. But they don't have the phone ringing, kids crying or religious zealots knocking on their door. So do yourself a favor! Don't try to put together a six-course meal in-between carpool trips. You'll go berserk. Save cooking special meals for when you know you have the time to do it right. Or why don't you call me? I love to travel!

When my catering business began, Cindy was right there giving me a jump start by always recommending me to her friends. When *Laverne & Shirley* achieved the pinnacle in TV ratings, I did many more parties for Cindy.

I particularly remember a fund-raiser for a remarkable woman, the late Bella Abzug, who was running for New York State Senate. Known as "Battling Bella," she was a civil rights lawyer and prominent peace campaigner who helped found the National Women's Political Caucus. Having won a seat in Congress, she was known for her outspoken views and her signature hats.

Liberals liked her and women throughout the country adored her. Especially Cindy, who asked me to donate my services for a luncheon being held at the Beverly Hills home of Emmy winners Renee Taylor (best known for her recent work as Fran Drescher's mom on the hit TV series *The Nanny*) and husband Joe Bologna. Renowned abstract artist Louise Nevelson agreed to donate a limited number of collages to be given those who made hefty-sized contributions.

Although the luncheon was a smashing success with Jane Fonda, Lily Tomlin, Valerie Harper and so many others in attendance, I was disappointed that Louise Nevelson wasn't there, as I admire her artwork tremendously.

There were no leftovers in any sense that afternoon. Not extra pasta, nor leftover collages. All the art work had been awarded to generous donors. I resigned myself to adding a Louise

Nevelson work to my list of wants.

Several weeks later I got a mysterious-sounding call from Cindy inviting me to her house. Upon arriving, I realized she was leading me to her bedroom. Once there I glanced about from her bed to the floor, where I discovered . . . the Nevelson collage. At the luncheon, Cindy had seen me admire the piece. Having received one for her donation, Cindy had decided to surprise me with hers as a way to say thank you for my efforts. To this day the piece adorns my living room, a lovely testament to our friendship.

Cindy helped me get my first break as an on-air caterer. She asked me to join her on *The Home Show* when host Gary Collins interviewed her at her home. The producers wanted to contrast Cindy's real-life digs with her role as a factory worker on *Laverne & Shirley*. I was there to prepare her favorite dish: Chicken Piccata. I was very nervous, but Cindy really calmed me. No, she didn't kick me, but I wouldn't be surprised if the thought occurred to her. She just kept telling me "You'll be *great!*" with such conviction. I don't know how I came off on camera, but I know one thing for sure, the Chicken Piccata was great.

STUFFED BREAST of VEAL
Serves 12

2 tablespoons olive oil
1 large onion
2 garlic cloves, minced
1 tablespoon dried marjoram, crumbled
2 tablespoons freshly chopped thyme
3 slices of homemade-type white bread, crusts removed
½ cup cream
1¼ pound mild Italian sausage, removed from casings
20 ounces frozen chopped spinach, thawed, drained and squeezed dry
2 teaspoons salt
2 tablespoon Dijon-style mustard
3 large eggs, lightly beaten
1 cup freshly grated Parmesan
1 whole 8 to 10-pound veal breast, halved crosswise by the butcher, leaving the meat on the bone, a deep pocket cut lengthwise in each half, leaving a 1-inch border on 3 sides
6 large eggs, hard-cooked
8 cups chicken stock or canned chicken broth
2 cups dry white wine
parsley for garnish

1) Heat the oil in a skillet, add the onion and cook, stirring until it is soft. Add the garlic, marjoram and thyme and cook the mixture for 2 minutes. Add the sausage meat and cook until lightly browned. Let the mixture cool.

2) Soak the bread in a bowl with the cream for 20 minutes, squeeze it dry and in a large bowl combine it with the spinach, salt, mustard, beaten eggs, Parmesan and the sausage-onion mixture.

3) In a food processor, blend mixture in batches only to a coarse puree, pulsing the motor. Taste for seasoning.

4) Sprinkle the pockets of each half of the veal breast lightly with salt and pepper. Coat the hard-cooked eggs with some of the stuffing and spread ¼ of the stuffing into each pocket. Arrange 3 of the eggs lengthwise down the center of the stuffing in each pocket, spacing them evenly, top with remaining stuffing and sew openings closed on each half with a trussing needle and kitchen string.

5) Wrap each half in a large piece of cheesecloth and securely tie the ends of the cheesecloth with kitchen string.

6) Preheat oven to 350°F. In a large saucepan bring the stock and the wine to a simmer. In each of 2 large baking pans, arrange the veal breast bone side up. Pour half of the stock mixture over each breast half. Braise the veal, cover tightly with foil and roast for 2 ½ to 3 hours or until the veal is tender.

7) Transfer the veal to a cutting board, reserving the stock for another use. Cut the bones from the veal in one piece and discard. Thinly slice the veal with a serrated knife, arrange it decoratively on a heated platter and garnish with sprigs of parsley. ✓

Everyone has a favorite way to ensure the turkey is juicy and tender. Some people swear by placing the bird in a paper bag that's moistened periodically, others use plastic roasting bags, while some cook the bird upside down at a very low temperature. I've been using a buttered cheesecloth method that my grandmother taught me. Over the years I've experimented with the other methods, but find the cheesecloth technique far superior.

OVEN-ROASTED TURKEY and ALL the TRIMMINGS
Serves 8

Corn Bread, Sausage and Mushroom Stuffing
2 links mild Italian sausage, casings removed, meat crumbled
2 large onions, chopped (about 4 cups)
6 ribs of celery chopped
½ cup unsalted butter (1 stick)
1 pound white mushrooms, thinly sliced
salt and pepper
6 cups packaged corn bread stuffing
1 tablespoon dried sage, crumbled

Turkey
1 14-pound turkey, exclude liver, reserve neck and giblets for stock
¾ cup (1½ sticks) unsalted butter, softened
1 cup chicken broth

Gravy
⅓ cup all-purpose flour
1 teaspoon paprika
4 cups turkey giblet stock (recipe to follow) or chicken broth
Fresh green leaves and red crabapples for garnish

1) Preheat oven to 425°F. In a large skillet, sauté the crumbled sausage meat and set aside. Sauté the onions and celery in butter over low heat until the vegetables are softened. Add the mushrooms in batches, stirring until cooked. Add salt and pepper.

2) In a bowl, combine the cooked mixture with the corn bread. Stir in the sage and salt and pepper to taste and toss together until well combined. Let cool.

3) Rinse the turkey inside and out. Pat dry and season with salt and pepper. Pack the neck cavity loosely with stuffing. Fold the neck skin under the body. Fill the body cavity loosely with the stuffing and tie the drumsticks together with kitchen string. Place any remaining stuffing in a buttered baking dish and reserve it covered and chilled.

4) Spread ½ stick of the butter over the turkey and roast it on a rack in a roasting pan in a preheated 425°F oven for 30 minutes.

5) In a saucepan, melt the remaining butter and let it cool. Reduce the oven temperature to 325°F and continue basting the turkey with the pan juices and drape it with a piece of cheesecloth soaked in the melted butter. Lift the cheesecloth and baste the turkey with the pan juices every 20 minutes for 2½ to 3 hours or until a meat thermometer inserted into the fleshy part of the thigh reads 180°F.

6) During the last hour, drizzle the reserved stuffing with the broth and ½ cup pan juices, cover loosely and bake.

7) Discard the cheesecloth and string from turkey and transfer the bird to a heated platter, reserving the juices in the pan. Let it stand loosely covered with foil for 25 minutes.

8) To make the gravy, skim all but ⅓ cup of the fat from the roasting pan. With a whisk, stir in flour and form a roux. Cook over moderate heat, whisking for 3-5 minutes. Add the paprika and cook the mixture for 30 seconds. Add the stock in a stream, whisking to a near boil. Add salt and pepper to taste. Stirring occasionally, slowly simmer the gravy for 12 minutes and serve in a heated sauceboat. Garnish the turkey with green leaves and crabapples and serve. ✓

Turkey Giblet Stock
Makes about 6 cups

giblets from the turkey, (excluding the liver),
  chopped
3 cups chicken broth
3 cups water
1 onion stuck with 3 cloves
1 rib of celery, chopped
1 carrot, halved
¼ teaspoon dried thyme
½ bay leaf
3 parsley sprigs

1) In a heavy-bottomed saucepan, combine the
giblets, the broth, the water, the onion, celery
and carrot and bring to a boil, skimming the
froth as it rises to the surface.

2) Add the thyme, bay leaf and parsley and cook
over moderate heat for 1 hour.

3) Strain the stock through a fine sieve, pressing
hard on the solids, and let it cool. Chill the
stock and remove the fat.

Country Ham Stuffing
Serves 8

½ cup (1 stick) unsalted butter
½ pound baked ham, cut into 1-inch cubes
2 large onions, chopped
6 ribs of celery, chopped
salt and pepper
4 cups crustless, day-old homestyle white bread,
  coarsely cut into cubes

¼ cup fresh parsley, chopped
1 teaspoon each of dried sage, rosemary and
  thyme
turkey giblet stock or chicken broth
½ cup of the pan juices from last hour of turkey
  roasting

1) In a large skillet, melt butter and sauté the
ham; add the onions, celery, and salt and pepper
to taste. Continue to sauté over low heat until
the vegetables are softened.

2) In a bowl, combine the cooked mixtures
with the bread cubes. Stir in the parsley, sage,
rosemary and thyme (singing optional) and
combine well. Let cool.

3) Preheat oven to 325°F. Place the stuffing in a
buttered casserole dish. Drizzle with turkey
giblet stock or chicken broth and pan juices.
Bake for 20 minutes.

**Cranberry, Shallot and
Dried-Cherry Compote**
Makes 6 to 7 cups

½ pound shallots (about 16, each about 1 inch
  in diameter)
1 tablespoon unsalted butter
¾ cup sugar
½ cup white-wine vinegar
1 cup dry white wine
½ teaspoon salt
1 cup dried, unsweetened sour cherries
2 cups fresh (picked over) or unthawed frozen
  cranberries
½ cup water

1) In a saucepan of boiling water, blanch shallots
1 minute and drain. Peel shallots and separate
into cloves where possible.

2) In a heavy saucepan, cook shallots in butter
over moderate heat, stirring, until well coated.
Add sugar and 1 tablespoon vinegar and cook,
stirring, until sugar mixture turns a golden
caramel.

3) Add remaining vinegar, wine and salt and
boil 1 minute. Add cherries and simmer,
covered, 45 minutes, or until shallots are tender.

4) Add cranberries and water and boil gently,
uncovered, stirring occasionally 10 minutes or
until cranberries burst. Transfer compote to a
bowl and cool. Compote may be made 5 days
ahead and chilled, covered. Serve at room
temperature. ✒

A Kitchen Comedy

There's a famous saying, "Behind every good man is a good woman." In my case, there have been several. One in particular is Beverly Hills facialist Nance "Matchmaker" Mitchell. Nance just loves putting people together. That's how I met Carrie Fisher.

Nance had arranged to have me visit her salon while Carrie was having a facial. Nance had given me a big buildup and I arrived with Carrie expecting me. She was charming, sweet, very down-to-earth with a hint of that brilliant wit shining through her herbal minted face mask. It was instant friendship and the start of many big laughs we would share, some of which I will reveal momentarily.

At the time, Carrie had completed her second of the *Star Wars* film trilogies and was flush with success. She was renting a rustic two-bedroom cottage with a small pool and enormous deck that overlooked Universal Studios. It was there I would prepare many parties.

One of the first was a Thanksgiving dinner that was romantic beyond plan. Carrie was dating music genius Paul Simon, who brought record impresario David Geffen. Actress Teri Garr came too. Carrie wanted an intimate meal, which turned out to be that and more. For just as everyone sat down to eat, a "brown out" or, literally, a power outage, occurred. Luckily, Carrie's stove was gas, so it didn't affect the meal. But I did pause to wonder how I would navigate the food from the kitchen to the table, as it was pitch black. While I endured fearful flashes of spilling the potatoes on Paul or gravy on David, Carrie rounded up her candle collection and we served the meal adorned by the warm glow of friendship and candlelight.

Carrie has an insatiable curiosity. After asking on several occasions how I prepared certain foods, she devised her own ingenious way to find out. How? She decided to combine her love of fine entertaining and cuisine by hosting a series of cooking classes led by *you know who*. Once a week, Carrie would gather five or six people for two hours to prepare a meal and at 9:00 PM about ten or more people would show up to devour it. You never knew what hungry souls would walk through the door – from Harrison Ford to Meryl Streep, Barbra Streisand, Woody Harrelson, Candice Bergen, Anjelica Houston and even Carrie's mom, Debbie Reynolds. We made Mexican, Italian, French . . . I even brought in a Chinese chef for some very special Mandarin meals. The cooking classes became a tradition at Carrie's and launched my "teaching" career that I continue to this day.

One of the people I met at Carrie's is Penny Marshall – the talented film director (my favorites are *Big*, *A League of Their Own*, and *Awakenings*) and actress-comedienne who first starred with my soulmate Cindy Williams in the TV series *Laverne & Shirley*. Because Penny and Carrie have a lot in common including their astrological signs (their birthdays are

a few days apart), they often celebrate together. On one of these occasions, a comical scene took place unbeknownst to them, that I think they'll enjoy hearing about.

The birthday party was held in the Hollywood Hills house Penny was renting from Gore Vidal. It was an old Med-iterranean, with a harem-style den and a huge raised pool and patio. It was in October and I was lucky enough to find some fabulous gardenias. I had them everywhere – in the house, by the food and floating in the pool. The fragrance was enchanting and very representative of Hollywood in the forties.

The focal point of the evening, besides the birthday girls, of course, was to be the cake. It was designed on a plate of glass and was to be illuminated from underneath with tiny white lights. The party was for 200 people and the cake was to serve *at least* that many. As a result, it was enormous. So big in fact, that . . .

When the pastry chef finished decor-ating, he asked two of us to help bring it outside. Carefully we started to lift this hefty confection only to be stopped short at the door. We couldn't get it through. Panic time. What to do? Cut it in half and reassemble? Tip it sideways and risk everything falling off? We tried every other opening out of the kitchen but with no success. I whipped out my tape measurer and took more measurements than a nearsighted carpenter. We began to laugh hysterically. I felt like I was in a sitcom like *I Love Lucy*, *Laverne & Shirley*, or better put, *The Three Stooges*. My first

The name of this pasta tastefully translated means "Ladies-of-the-Night Spaghetti." Legend has it that when street-walking ladies prepared dinner, they would combine whatever they had in their cupboards. This dish evolved.

SPAGHETTI alla PUTTANESCA
Serves 6

¼ cup olive oil
1 tablespoon finely minced garlic
4 cups peeled, chopped tomatoes, preferably
  fresh, or imported Italian plum tomatoes
⅓ cup finely chopped parsley
2 tablespoons finely chopped fresh basil
1 teaspoon dried oregano
½ teaspoon red pepper flakes, or more to taste
2 tablespoons drained capers
18 imported black olives, pitted
2 2-ounce cans flat anchovies
1 pound imported spaghetti, cooked al dente

1) Heat the oil in a deep heavy skillet. Add the garlic and without browning it, cook for about 30 seconds. Add the tomatoes, half of the parsley, the basil, oregano, red pepper flakes, capers and olives. Cook over moderately high heat for about 25 minutes, stirring frequently.

2) Drain the anchovies and chop coarsely.

3) When the sauce is ready, add the anchovies and remaining parsley and cook, stirring, for about 1 minute. Serve piping hot with freshly cooked spaghetti. This pesto sauce can be prepared in advance. Spoon it into a plastic container or freezer jar, filling the container almost to the brim. Seal and freeze. Defrost overnight in the refrigerator the day before serving. Heat gently. ✍

Spaghetti alla Puttanesca

major catastrophe! How could this happen? We decided to grit our teeth and pick up the glass and tip it sideways in hopes gravity would take a respite. There was no other way. At the count of three, we each held our breath and hoisted the plate and cake, tipping it sideways, squeezed through the door and made it through . . . only to see that the decorations were now off the cake and generously smeared on the door molding. Fortunately the pastry chef was able to redecorate it. And what we couldn't repair we patched with *gardenias!* It was enjoyed by Jack Nicholson, Kate Jackson, Cheech & Chong, Debbie Reynolds and many more, who didn't know the difference!

I didn't make the cake, so the recipe doesn't follow. However, equally delicious was the Spaghetti alla Puttanesca I prepared, which fortunately presented no problems in preparation, nor in getting it to the buffet table. ✓

RIGATONI with BROCCOLI and TOMATO in PESTO SAUCE
Serves 4

Pesto Sauce (recipe follows)
1 bunch of broccoli
salt
1 pound rigatoni or any tubular pasta, preferably
  imported
3 tablespoons olive oil
1 clove garlic, finely chopped
½ teaspoon or more hot red pepper flakes,
  optional
1 firm ripe red tomato

1) Prepare the Pesto Sauce and set aside.

2) Cut the broccoli into small florets. Trim the stalks and stems of the broccoli and cut into bite-size lengths. Steam the broccoli pieces over boiling water or cook in boiling salted water until crisp-tender. Do not overcook! Set aside.

3) Cook the rigatoni in boiling salted water to package directions, but take care not to overcook. The pasta must be tender and in no sense mushy. Reserve 1 to 2 tablespoons of the boiling pasta water before draining.

4) Heat the oil in a saucepan and add the garlic and blanched broccoli. Sprinkle with pepper flakes. Cook, stirring gently, just to heat through. Remove from heat.

5) Core tomato and cut into bite-size wedges.

6) Put the rigatoni in a bowl. Add the 1 to 2 tablespoons of the hot pasta water to the pesto and stir until slightly thinned. Do not make it soupy. Pour this mixture over the rigatoni adding salt to taste. Add the broccoli and tomato and toss to blend. Serve at room temperature.

Pesto Sauce
Yields enough sauce for 1 pound of pasta

2 cups fresh basil
½ cup olive oil
2 tablespoons pine nuts
2 cloves garlic, peeled
salt to taste
½ cup grated Parmesan cheese
2 tablespoons grated pecorino Romano cheese
3 tablespoons butter at room temperature
2 or 3 tablespoons cream cheese (optional)

1) Remove all stems from the basil. Then measure by packing the leaves gently but somewhat firmly in a measuring cup without crushing the leaves.

2) Empty the basil into a food processor or blender. Add the olive oil, pine nuts, garlic and salt and blend on high speed using a rubber spatula to scrape the sides down occasionally so that it blends evenly.

3) Pour the mixture into a bowl and beat in the grated cheeses by hand. Beat in the softened butter and the cream cheese (if desired).

4) Let stand until the sauce is at room temperature. ✓

This is one of those recipes that can be made in stages. I like to chop the vegetables several hours in advance, then wrap and refrigerate until later. I especially like using petite frozen peas for their sweetness. If you can't find them, use fresh peas, cook them unshelled with the asparagus and shell just before adding. For variation, add 1 pound of cooked, shelled shrimp when you prepare the pea-ham mixture.

PASTA PRIMAVERA with GARLIC BREAD
Serves 10 as a co-star or 8 as a starring dish

4 tablespoons unsalted butter
1 medium onion, minced
1 large garlic clove, minced
1 pound thin asparagus, ends trimmed, cut
    diagonally in ¼-inch slices with tips left intact
½ pound mushrooms, thinly sliced
6 ounces cauliflower, broken into small florets
1 medium zucchini, cut into ¼-inch rounds
1 small carrot halved lengthwise, cut diagonally
    into ⅛-inch slices
1 cup whipping cream
½ cup chicken stock
2 tablespoons chopped fresh basil
1 cup frozen petite peas
2 ounces prosciutto or cooked ham, chopped
5 green onions chopped
salt and freshly ground pepper to taste
1 pound assorted pasta cooked al dente,
    thoroughly drained
1 cup freshly grated imported Parmesan cheese

1) Melt the butter in a large deep skillet over medium-high heat. Add onion and garlic and sauté until onion is softened, about 2 minutes. Add asparagus, mushrooms, cauliflower, zucchini and carrot slices and stir-fry for 2 minutes. Remove several pieces of asparagus tips, mushrooms and zucchini and reserve for garnish.

2) Increase the heat to high and add cream, stock and basil and allow mixture to boil until liquid is slightly reduced, about 3 minutes. Stir in peas, ham and green onions and cook 1 minute more. Season to taste with salt and pepper.

3) Add pasta and cheese, tossing until thoroughly combined and pasta is heated through. Turn onto a large serving platter and garnish with reserved vegetables.

Garlic Bread
Serves 6

¼ cup (½ stick) unsalted butter at room
    temperature
1 tablespoon olive oil
2 garlic cloves, minced
1 tablespoon minced fresh parsley leaves
salt and pepper
1 14-inch loaf of Italian bread, cut horizontally
    in half

1) Preheat the oven to 350°F. In a bowl, combine the butter, oil, garlic, parsley, salt and pepper to taste.

2) Spread the mixture over the two halves of

bread. Close the bread halves together and wrap in foil.

3) Heat the bread for 10 minutes. Open the foil and open the bread halves with the cut sides facing upward. Heat for 5 more minutes. Cut into 1-inch slices and serve. ✓

To keep bread warm at the table, heat a ceramic tile in a hot oven for at least 30 minutes and place it on the bottom of your serving basket. Cover with a napkin, add the warm rolls and cover again.

Nick's Tip!

83

2) Add the wine, cook until evaporated and turn off the heat. Remove the garlic.

3) Cook the spaghetti in abundant boiling salted water until al dente.

4) While the spaghetti is cooking, lightly beat the egg yolks, add half-and-half and Parmesan, then combine with the cooked spaghetti and add to the sauté pan. Heat lightly and toss, being careful not to cook the eggs. Season with plenty of black pepper and sprinkle with parsley. Toss and serve immediately. ✐

I like to make this recipe with pancetta, an Italian bacon found in fine stores. You may use regular bacon but the search for pancetta is more than worth it.

SPAGHETTI CARBONARA
Serves 6

2 tablespoons extra-virgin olive oil
1 tablespoon unsalted butter
3 garlic cloves, peeled and crushed
1½ teaspoons red pepper flakes (optional)
½ pound pancetta cut into ¼-inch pieces

¼ cup dry white wine
1 pound imported spaghetti
4 large egg yolks
¾ cup freshly grated Parmesan cheese
freshly ground black pepper
handful of finely chopped Italian parsley
¼ to ½ cup half-and-half

1) In a sauté pan large enough to hold the pasta, combine the extra-virgin olive oil, butter, garlic, red pepper flakes and pancetta and sauté over low heat until pancetta renders its fat.

MANICOTTI
Serves 6-8

Crepes

4 eggs
1 cup sifted all-purpose flour
1 cup water
salt
vegetable oil

1) Break 3 of the eggs into a mixing bowl and beat well with a whisk or a fork. Add the flour slowly, beating constantly. Add the water, beating and stirring to make a smooth batter, and salt to taste.

2) Heat a small crepe pan about 5 inches in diameter. Brush with vegetable oil and add 2 tablespoons of the batter at a time. Swirl the crepe pan until a thin layer of batter covers the pan. Cook the crepes on 1 side only until they are set. Do not let them brown. Cook each crepe for a minute or so. When they are done, transfer them to a piece of waxed paper. The first couple of crepes don't turn out perfectly as the pan takes time to get seasoned. Keep going! Finish the batter. Stack crepes between pieces of waxed paper.

Tomato Sauce

3 tablespoons olive oil
1½ cups finely chopped yellow onion
1 clove garlic, minced
1 cup hearty red wine
1 29-ounce can Italian plum tomatoes
3 tablespoons tomato paste
1½ cups water
salt and freshly ground pepper to taste
2 sprigs fresh thyme or ½ teaspoon dried
4 basil leaves, coarsely chopped or
   1 teaspoon dried
1 bay leaf
1 tablespoon finely chopped Italian parsley

1) In a kettle, heat the oil and cook the onion and the garlic until wilted. Add the wine and simmer until evaporated. Add remaining ingredients and simmer, stirring occasionally, about 30 minutes. This sauce freezes well.

Filling

½ pound ricotta cheese
¼ pound mozzarella cheese, cut into ⅛-inch
   cubes
¼ cup freshly grated Parmesan cheese
2 tablespoons finely chopped Italian parsley
salt and freshly ground black pepper

In a mixing bowl, combine the ricotta, mozzarella, remaining egg, Parmesan cheese, parsley and salt and pepper to taste.

To Assemble the Manicotti:

1) Place 1 crepe uncooked side up on a flat surface. Add 1 or 2 tablespoons of filling and roll the crepe cigarette fashion. Arrange the manicotti in a greased baking dish. (Manicotti may be assembled in advance, covered and refrigerated.)

2) Spoon a generous amount of the tomato sauce over the manicotti. Bake 15-20 minutes until piping hot and serve. ✐

85

Nick's Tip!

A smashingly successful way to loosen garlic cloves from the bulb is to gently crush the whole bulb against your work surface. A good whack will snap the cloves from the root. To peel the garlic, gently smash the individual clove with a knife or cleaver and once broken, the skins will pull away easily.

A Fond Farewell

In 1992, Elizabeth Taylor offered her home to her friend Norma Heyman as a place to recuperate after surgery. I've known Norma as long as I've known Elizabeth, so it was a double pleasure when Elizabeth asked me to cook during Norma's stay. She's a longtime fan of my cooking, just as I am an admirer of the movies she's produced, especially *Dangerous Liaisons*.

One day I was walking by Norma's room on my way to the kitchen (where else?) when she cheerfully called out for me to come meet her friends. She introduced me to her son David and a woman named Lee who was wearing a rather festive straw hat and sitting in a chair next to her husband, "Doc." They had all come to check on Norma.

After the introductions, Norma praised my culinary skills. Elated by her compliments, I headed back to the kitchen when I was hit with the disturbing revelation that the lady in the hat was Lee Remick. It was unsettling because there was so little resemblance to the star I knew in *Anatomy of a Murder* or *Days of Wine and Roses* and many other films that suddenly flashed before me. In fact, the strikingly beautiful baton-twirling teenager who made her film debut in *A Face in the Crowd* now held a cane. It was hard to imagine this was the same woman who loved to sing and dance and dreamt of being in Broadway

gingeredSalmon

GINGERED SALMON
Serves 8-10

4 pounds salmon fillet, skin, bones and brown fat discarded

Marinade

4½ tablespoons minced green onions
3 tablespoons finely grated peeled fresh ginger root
3 tablespoons vegetable oil
¼ cup soy sauce
1 tablespoon sugar
1 tablespoon mirin (sweet rice wine available at Asian markets and some fine supermarkets)
1 tablespoon Oriental sesame oil
⅛ teaspoon black pepper

1) In a small skillet, cook the onion and ginger root in the vegetable oil over moderate heat, stirring until the mixture is golden. Remove the skillet from the heat.

2) In a bowl whisk together the soy, sugar, mirin, sesame oil, pepper and the scallion mixture. (The marinade can be made 2 weeks in advance and kept covered and chilled.)

Salmon

1) Arrange the salmon in a large shallow glass dish, spoon the marinade over it, and let the salmon marinate, covered and chilled, for at least 1 hour or overnight.

2) Preheat the broiler. Transfer the salmon with tongs to the rack of a foil-lined broiler pan. Brush generously with the marinade and broil about 4 inches from the heat for 5 minutes per ½ inch of thickness or until fish just flakes. (It is not necessary to turn the salmon.) Serve immediately.

I love this salmon recipe. Serve it with lemon wedges and sauces such as Mustard Mayonnaise, Anchovy Mayonnaise and Mustard Dill Sauce. Accompany with Cucumber Salad with Dill. Yes, making your own mayonnaise isn't as easy as buying it, but store-bought mayonnaise can't compare to the fresh, subtle flavor of homemade. If you're in an area where egg safety is an issue, use an egg substitute such as Egg Beaters as noted.

POACHED SALMON
Serves 12 as a main dish, 24 as an appetizer

Court Bouillon
24 cups water
1 bottle dry white wine
1½ cups coarsely chopped carrots
1½ cups coarsely chopped celery
3 cups chopped onions
4 cloves garlic, unpeeled but cut in half
1 hot red pepper
10 dill sprigs
6 sprigs fresh parsley
salt to taste
1 bay leaf
1½ cups coarsely chopped leeks
1 whole, cleaned, boned salmon, up to 7½ pounds
or
1 large section of salmon, such as the tail section or center cut, about 3½ pounds
Garnish of tarragon sprigs, halved cherry tomatoes, Boston lettuce, quartered small tomatoes, hard-cooked egg wedges, lemon wedges

1) Combine all the ingredients for the Court

musicals. For she was large. Hers wasn't the kind of heaviness that comes from overeating, but the bloat of serious illness. My heart sank.

Just then Elizabeth passed me and noticed I looked dazed. Gently she inquired what was wrong as I faced her, dumbfounded. Without my ever having to say a word, Elizabeth looked into my eyes and replied sympathetically that cancer is indeed merciless.

The next day while packing to leave, Norma told me that Lee's illness was in its final stage. Norma and Lee's extended families were providing moral support at Lee's home, taking turns cooking for her and Doc. Norma asked if I would come to the house and make Louisiana Baked Shrimp. I was honored and agreed immediately.

Several days later I went to Lee's home on a residential street in Brentwood. Very country-like and unpretentious, it was a joyful, cheerful house. Although she was now in a wheelchair, Lee was nevertheless very excited as her house-keeper wheeled her into the big family-style kitchen to watch me cook. She was torn between learning how to make this dish that Norma had raved about and watching the Boston Red Sox on TV. But I was no competition for the Sox. She gradually made her way to the den where I could hear her shouting team encouragements.

I left that night with the sound of cheering in my ears. Voices of team spirit were championing a win. Full of enthusiasm and hope for the moment. Driving down San Vicente Boulevard as the sun kissed the ocean goodnight, I could still hear echoes of Lee's cheers and for a second saw that baton-twirling beauty spiritedly rallying her team to a valiant victory. ✐

Bouillon in a fish cooker or a kettle large enough to hold the fish. Bring to a boil and simmer covered for about 20 minutes. Let cool.

2) Wrap the whole salmon or piece in cheesecloth or a clean towel and tie neatly with string. Lower it into the fish cooker and cover. Bring to a boil and simmer gently for 20 minutes. (The cooking time is the same for a whole salmon or a large center section.) Let stand briefly and serve hot, or let cool completely until ready to use if it is to be served at room temperature.

3) Remove the salmon and untie it. Remove the cheesecloth or towel. Place the salmon carefully on a flat surface and pull and scrap away the skin. Scrape away the thin dark brown flesh that coats the main pink flesh.

4) Decorate and garnish the salmon as desired. You may wish to drop large tarragon sprigs in boiling water, drain immediately, then chill in ice water. Pat leaves dry. Garnish surface of salmon with tarragon leaves and halved cherry tomatoes. Around the salmon, arrange small Boston lettuce cups filled with hard-cooked egg wedges neatly placed between quartered small tomatoes.

Quick Homemade Mayonnaise
Makes about 1 cup

1 large egg★
5 teaspoons fresh lemon juice
1 teaspoon Dijon-style mustard
¼ teaspoon salt
¼ teaspoon white pepper
1 cup olive oil

★Use ½ cup Egg Beaters and increase lemon juice to 10 teaspoons total.

In a blender with the machine running on high speed, blend the egg, lemon juice, mustard, salt and the white pepper. Add oil in a slow stream.

Mustard Mayonnaise

Follow the Quick Homemade Mayonnaise recipe, adding 2 or 3 tablespoons of coarse-grained mustard, or to taste.

Anchovy Mayonnaise

Follow the Quick Homemade Mayonnaise recipe, adding 3 flat anchovy fillets, rinsed, drained and patted dry.

Cranberry Mayonnaise

Follow the Quick Homemade Mayonnaise recipe, adding 4 heaping tablespoons of pureed Cranberry, Shallot and Dried-Cherry Compote (see page 78), 1 tablespoon fresh lime juice, salt and pepper to taste. Chill 1 hour before using. ✐

Nick's Tip!

While you're at it, make a face mask for yourself with this recipe from Beverly Hills facialist Nance Mitchell. For oily skin, mix two egg whites. For dry skin, mix two egg yolks. Normal skin, two whole eggs. Keep the mask on until it dries, then remove with a damp washcloth. This way you'll have delicious mayonnaise *and* have skin that looks as beautiful as any of Nance's celebrity clients!

The French method of cooking a fillet of fish wrapped in parchment creates a flash-steaming process. This technique yields a dramatic presentation when opened at the table as the steam and aromas come billowing out.

FRESH ORANGE ROUGHY en PAPILLOTE
Per individual portion

4 medium mushrooms, thinly sliced
1 8-ounce fillet of orange roughy
   (halibut, pompano, sea bass and red snapper
   can be substituted)
salt
freshly ground pepper
3 tablespoons tomato concasse (peeled, seeded
   and finely chopped ripe tomatoes)
1 tablespoon unsalted butter
4 small sprigs of coriander, tarragon or Italian
   parsley
1 tablespoon dry white wine
lemon juice or lemon slices
aluminum foil, or parchment, available at fine
   cooking stores

1) Preheat oven to 450°F. Cut large sheets of foil (or parchment) into individual 15-inch squares.

2) Arrange a bed of mushrooms in the center of the foil (parchment) and lay fish on top, then season with salt and pepper, arrange tomatoes on top, then add butter and herbs. Sprinkle with wine or lemon juice or put sliced lemons on top.

3) Fold foil (parchment) in half over the fish and seal the edges so the package will not leak.

Bake for 10 minutes. Open package and serve immediately. This may be prepared early and refrigerated until time to cook. ✓

Tuna tastes better raw than cooked. It has a meaty taste similar to beef, so for this recipe I recommend undercooking the fish. This particular dish dates back probably to early Roman times when the fish was pulled from the Mediterranean Sea surrounding Sicily, then cleaned and grilled. The success of this recipe depends entirely on the quality of the fish, so when shopping insist upon the finest sashimi tuna.

GRILLED FILLET of FRESH TUNA with SHALLOT and PINE NUT SAUCE
Per individual portion

1 6-ounce piece fresh tuna, cut 1-inch thick
lemon wedges

Tuna Marinade

½ cup olive oil
juice of ½ lemon
fresh or dried oregano to taste
salt and freshly ground black pepper

1) Mix together the olive oil, lemon juice and oregano. Salt and pepper the fish and add to the olive oil mixture and marinate for at least ½ hour at room temperature.

2) Heat the coals until gray. Grill the fish 8 inches from the coals for 5 minutes, basting often with a sprig of oregano. Turn once and continue basting for another 5 minutes, being sure not to overcook. Serve immediately with Shallot and Pine Nut Sauce.

Shallot and Pine Nut Sauce
for 2 servings

½ cup shallots, finely chopped
½ cup hazelnut oil
2 tablespoons medium-dry sherry
3 tablespoons plus 1 teaspoon raspberry vinegar
2 teaspoons Dijon-style mustard
½ teaspoon coarse salt
2 teaspoons freshly ground black pepper
¼ cup pine nuts, toasted
¼ cup minced flat-leaf parsley

1) While the fish is marinating, make the sauce in a small skillet, cooking the shallots in 2 tablespoons of the oil over moderately low heat, swirling the skillet until shallots are softened.

2) In a bowl, whisk together the sherry, vinegar, mustard, salt and pepper and then add the remaining 6 tablespoons of oil in a stream, whisking until sauce is emulsified. Whisk in shallots, pine nuts and parsley. Serve the sauce with the grilled fish.

This sauce can also be used with grilled chicken and grilled vegetables. ✓

OrangeRoughy *et papillote*

GRILLED SWORDFISH with BASIL BUTTER
Serves 4

4 6-ounce pieces of swordfish
lemon wedges
Basil Butter (recipe follows)

Marinade
½ cup olive oil
juice of 1 lemon
fresh or dried oregano to taste
salt and freshly ground black pepper

1) Combine ingredients and marinate the fish
for at least 1 hour or longer, covered and
refrigerated. Reserve marinade for basting.

2) Heat the coals to gray. Grill the fish 8 inches
from the coals, basting often with the marinade.
Turn once and continue basting. Be sure not to
overcook. Fish is done when it flakes easily. Spread
with the Basil Butter and serve immediately.

Basil Butter
Makes almost 1 cup

2 cloves of garlic, unpeeled
¾ cup firmly packed fresh basil leaves
½ cup (1 stick) unsalted butter
1 teaspoon Dijon-style mustard
1 teaspoon grated lemon rind
freshly ground white pepper and salt to taste

1) Boil the cloves of garlic for 10 minutes and
let them cool. Blanch the basil leaves in the
same water for 10 seconds. Drain the basil well.
Pat dry and mince it.

2) In a bowl, cream the butter, the peeled and
mashed garlic, the basil, the mustard, lemon
rind, pepper and salt. Cover with plastic wrap
and store chilled overnight. ✓

*Some people think you need to be a real gourmet to
prepare shrimp. Well, you don't! This recipe is easy,
elegant and always a hit. If you want to make it for
shrimps (I mean kids), just omit the cayenne. And if
you're counting calories, reduce the butter to 1/2
tablespoon, or omit completely.*

LOUISIANA BAKED SHRIMP
Serves 2

¾ pound (about 15) large shrimp, shelled
  and deveined
3 tablespoons unsalted butter
1 teaspoon chili powder
1 teaspoon freshly ground black pepper
⅛ teaspoon cayenne
1 teaspoon minced garlic
1 tablespoon Worcestershire sauce
2 tablespoons red wine
¼ teaspoon salt
crusty French bread

1) Preheat oven to 400°F. Arrange the shrimp in
a baking dish just large enough for 1 layer.

2) In a small saucepan, combine the butter, chili
powder, black pepper, cayenne, garlic,
Worcestershire sauce, wine and salt. Bring the
mixture to a boil and pour over the shrimp.

3) Bake the shrimp uncovered for 8 to 10
minutes or until they are just firm.

Serve with bread on the side. ✓

*This is one of my favorite pastas because it is so
fresh, simple and quick to prepare. Italians rarely add
Parmesan cheese to a fish pasta, so you won't find it
suggested here. I do, however, love to add lots of
freshly ground black pepper.*

SHRIMP and FRESH TUNA PASTA
Serves 6

4 to 6 tablespoons extra-virgin olive oil
¾ pound shrimp, shelled and deveined
1 pound fresh tuna, cut into 1-inch strips
salt and pepper
2 cloves garlic, finely chopped
2 cups shelled fresh peas
¾ cup crème fraîche pg. 115
1 handful fresh basil leaves cut into narrow
  ribbons, saving a few for garnish
1 pound imported spaghetti

1) In a large skillet, heat olive oil over
moderately high heat and sauté the shrimp and
tuna. Season with salt and pepper. After a
minute, lower the heat and add the garlic and
peas and cook for 1 minute.

2) Add the crème fraîche and basil and cook for
another minute or so.

3) Cook pasta separately, according to package
directions. Drain and add to the skillet. Mix
well, taste for seasoning and serve garnished
with a few fresh basil leaves. ✓

92

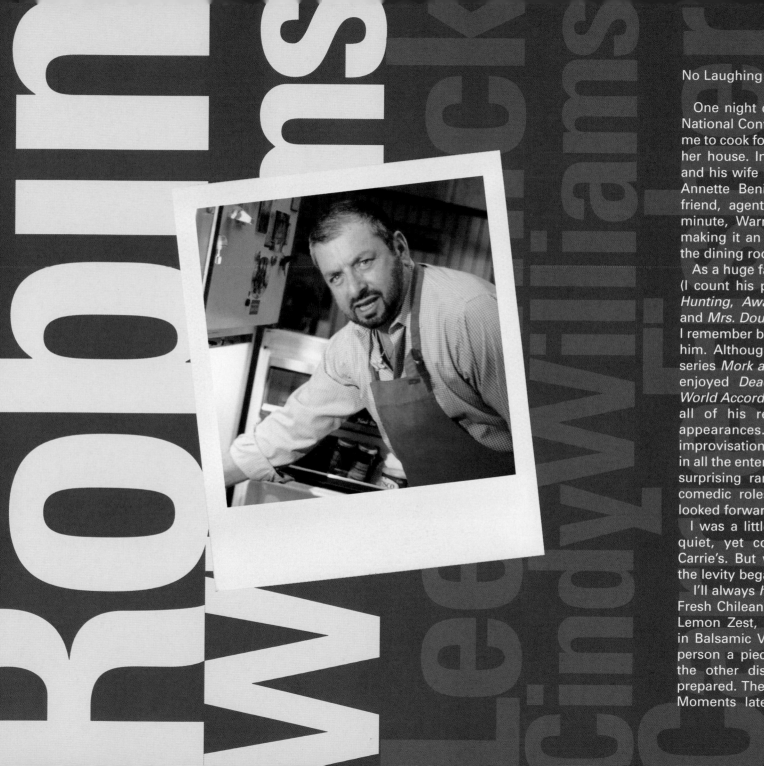

No Laughing Matter

One night during the 1992 Republican National Convention, Carrie Fisher asked me to cook for an intimate dinner party at her house. Invited were Robin Williams and his wife Marsha, Warren Beatty and Annette Bening and Carrie's then-best friend, agent Bryan Lourd. At the last minute, Warren and Annette canceled, making it an informal dinner for four in the dining room.

As a huge fan of Robin Williams's work (I count his performances in *Good Will Hunting*, *Awakenings*, *The Fisher King* and *Mrs. Doubtfire* among my favorites) I remember being curious about meeting him. Although I had never seen his TV series *Mork and Mindy*, I had very much enjoyed *Dead Poets Society* and *The World According to Garp*. Not to mention all of his records, concerts and TV appearances. His bounty of brilliant improvisational manic riffs were plentiful in all the entertainment arenas as was his surprising range in both dramatic and comedic roles. For all these reasons I looked forward to meeting him.

I was a little surprised to find him so quiet, yet completely comfortable at Carrie's. But with the advent of dinner the levity began to rise.

I'll always *hear* that menu in my mind: Fresh Chilean Sea Bass, Snap Peas with Lemon Zest, and Potatoes with Onions in Balsamic Vinegar. First I served each person a piece of fish while describing the other dishes and how they were prepared. Then I returned to the kitchen. Moments later, I reentered the dining room where Robin was speaking in a very efficient voice, pointing out the vegetables, the fish . . . the entire meal. Instantly, I realized he was mimicking me. He was a human tape recorder playing back a caricatured rendition of me. It was completely disarming. After all, I've had people copy my recipes, but never my voice, my style, my . . . "me-ness."

"Well," I said jokingly, "if you're going to do *my* lines, does that mean I get to do *yours* on your next film?"

Robin flashed the childlike smile of a kid whose hand had been caught in the cookie jar, while Marsha said she thought it was an excellent idea. Besides, I could go to Kenya – his next destination.

Following dinner, everyone adjourned to watch the televised convention. All eyes were seriously glued to the set. Familiar with Carrie's and Robin's well-known wit, I readily anticipated the sarcastic asides. But there was only the sound of silence from those viewing the proceedings. The air was thick with concentration. When it came time for Dan Quayle's speech, I braced myself for a machine-gun spraying of Robin's quips. All throughout the Reagan/Quayle term, he never missed an opportunity to publicly make a Dan Quayle crack. But tonight was different. Our country's future was possibly being foreshadowed by the convention's speakers. And this was no laughing matter. In fact, no one made a single joke or dig. All were completely engrossed in what Quayle had to say. On this night, when the Vice-President spoke, the people *listened*. That is, except for me. I returned to the kitchen. ✍

94

Here's a fish recipe that's ideal for dieters. Low in calories and cholesterol, it's especially tasty and easy to prepare thanks to Chef Paul Prudhomme's "Seafood Magic" Seasoning Blends. It's got all my favorite spices in one bottle and does not contain any MSG, sugar, additives or preservatives. Available at most major supermarkets.

FRESH CHILEAN SEA BASS
Serves 4

1 3-pound fillet fresh Chilean sea bass (do NOT use individual pieces)
Chef Paul Prudhomme's "Seafood Magic" to taste
lemon wedges

1) Preheat oven to 375°F. Spray a cookie sheet with a nonstick cooking spray.

2) Place the fillet on the pan and then spray the top of the fish with the non-stick spray. Generously sprinkle the Seafood Magic on top.

3) Bake until flaky, about 20-30 minutes. Serve immediately and garnish with lemon wedges. ✍

PRIME RIB of BEEF with PORCINI PAN GRAVY and YORKSHIRE PUDDING
Serves 8-10

1 4-rib standing beef rib roast (weighing approximately 10 pounds trimmed)
1 teaspoon salt
1 tablespoon fresh rosemary leaves
½ cup (1 stick) plus 1½ tablespoons unsalted butter, softened

1 onion, chopped
1 green bell pepper, chopped
1 ounce dried porcini mushrooms
2 cups hot water
¼ pound fresh mushrooms, sliced
2½ cups beef broth
½ cup medium dry sherry
4 teaspoons arrowroot dissolved in 1½ tablespoons cold water
1 bunch fresh rosemary sprig for garnish

1) Preheat oven to 500°F. Keep the rib roast at room temperature for at least 1 hour. In a bowl, knead together the salt, rosemary and ½ stick butter and rub the meat with the mixture.

2) In a roasting pan, roast the meat with the rib side down for 30 minutes. Reduce the heat to 350°F and continue roasting for 1½ to 2 hours or until a meat thermometer inserted registers 130°F for medium-rare meat.

3) After the meat has been cooking 1 hour and 45 minutes, add the onion and bell pepper.

4) Soak the porcini mushrooms in the hot water for 30 minutes and using your hand, squeeze out any excess liquid, reserving it in the bowl. Discard the stems and thinly slice the caps. Strain the reserved liquid into a bowl through a fine sieve lined with cheesecloth.

5) Transfer the roast to a heated platter. Discard the string from the roast. Drain the onion and the bell pepper on paper towels and reserve them for the porcini gravy. Let the roast stand 15 to 20 minutes before carving.

6) In a heavy skillet, sauté the fresh mushrooms in the remaining butter over moderately high heat, stirring for 1 minute. Add the porcini mushrooms and continue sautéing the mixture, stirring for 1 minute. Add the broth and the reserved mushroom liquid. Boil the liquid until reduced to about 2 cups.

7) Skim all but 1 tablespoon of the fat from the pan juices in the roasting pan. Add the reserved pepper and onion with the sherry and sauté the mixture over medium-high heat, scraping up any browned bits. Boil the sherry mixture until reduced by ½.

8) Strain the pan juice mixture through a fine sieve into the mushroom mixture and bring it all to a boil. Stir the arrowroot mixture and add to the gravy. Simmer the gravy for 4 minutes, stirring constantly. Add salt and pepper to taste and transfer the gravy to a heated sauceboat. Serve the roast garnished with fresh rosemary sprigs and the pan gravy.

Yorkshire Pudding
Serves 8

1 cup milk at room temperature
2 large eggs at room temperature
¾ teaspoon salt
1 cup all-purpose flour
¼ cup reserved rib roast pan drippings

1) In a blender, combine the milk, eggs and salt and blend for 15 seconds. With the motor running, add the flour, a little at a time, and blend the mixture at high speed for 2 minutes.

Let the batter stand in the blender at room temperature for 3 hours.

2) Preheat oven to 450°F. In a 10-inch cast-iron skillet, heat the reserved drippings in the preheated oven for 10 minutes, or until it is just smoking. Blend the batter at high speed for 10 seconds and pour it into the skillet.

3) Bake the pudding in the middle of the oven for 20 minutes. Reduce the heat to 350°F and bake the pudding for 10 more minutes.

4) Transfer the pudding to a platter and serve immediately. ✍

TENDERLOIN of BEEF with MADEIRA SAUCE
Serves 6

4-pound tenderloin fillet of beef
1 clove garlic, crushed and made into a paste
salt and pepper to taste
½ cup (1 stick) unsalted butter
½ cup Madeira
2 cups brown beef stock

1) Have your butcher completely trim a 4-pound tenderloin fillet of beef and tie it in 2 or 3 places. Using your hands, spread the garlic and plenty of salt and pepper over the meat.

2) Preheat oven to 450°F. Melt ½ stick butter in a heavy ovenproof skillet over high heat. Brown the meat on all sides.

3) Place beef on rack in the oven, basting with the melted butter every 5 minutes for approximately 25 minutes for rare meat, depending upon the thickness of the fillet. Transfer the meat to a cutting board and let it stand for 10 minutes.

4) Pour all but 2 tablespoons of fat from the pan and add the Madeira. Deglaze the pan over moderately high heat, scraping up the brown bits clinging to the bottom and sides. Add the beef stock, stir, and strain the mixture into a saucepan. Bring the mixture to a boil and cook over moderately high heat until it is reduced to 1½ cups. Remove the pan from the heat and swirl in the remaining ½ stick of butter that has been softened and cut into pieces.

5) Cut the meat into ¾-inch slices and arrange overlapping on a heated platter. Spoon some of the sauce over the slices and serve the remaining sauce in a sauceboat. ✍

95

MOUSSAKA
Serves 10-12

3 eggplants
salt and pepper
2 pounds ground beef
¼ cup (½ stick) unsalted butter
2 onions
1 garlic clove
¼ teaspoon cinnamon
½ teaspoon nutmeg
½ teaspoon *fines herbes*
2 tablespoons parsley
1 8-ounce can tomato sauce
½ cup red wine
olive oil for brushing skillet
grated Parmesan to taste
4 cups Béchamel Sauce (recipe follows)

1) Preheat oven to 350°F. Peel and cut the eggplants lengthwise into ½-inch slices and sprinkle with salt, setting aside on paper towels to absorb the moisture.

2) Heat the butter and sauté the ground beef with salt and pepper, onions and garlic, crumbling the meat with a fork. When the meat is evenly browned, add ¼ teaspoon of cinnamon, ¼ teaspoon nutmeg, *fines herbes*, parsley and tomato sauce. Stir mixture well. Add wine and simmer for 20 minutes.

3) Wipe the salted eggplant. Lightly oil the skillet with a pastry brush and quick-fry the eggplant over very high heat; lay on paper towels to drain.

4) In a greased 9x13x2-inch baking pan, place a layer of eggplant topped with meat mixture and sprinkle with cheese. Cover remaining eggplant with cheese and Béchamel Sauce. Top with ¼ teaspoon grated nutmeg and lots of grated cheese. Bake for 1 hour.

5) When cool, cut into 3-inch squares and serve.

Béchamel Sauce

6 tablespoons butter
½ cup all-purpose flour
3 cups low-fat milk
salt and freshly grated nutmeg
3 egg yolks (optional)★

1) In a heavy-bottomed saucepan, melt the butter over low and steady heat. (Make sure the sauce thickens without burning.)

2) When the butter has reached a frothing point, add the flour. With a wooden spoon, mix well and cook until golden brown. (★For richer sauce, add 3 egg yolks now.) Remove the pan from the heat and let it rest about 15 minutes.

3) Warm the milk until it is close to boiling. Return the butter/flour mixture to the heat and very quickly pour in the hot milk. Do not pour it slowly, as it will create lumps. Mix with a wooden spoon as you pour, stirring in the same direction to prevent lumps. When the sauce boils, add salt and nutmeg. Reduce heat and cook 12 to 15 minutes stirring gently. Remove from the heat and cover until needed. ✒

ROSEMARY RACK of LAMB
Serves 4

2 7-rib racks of lamb weighing about 1¼
   pounds each, trimmed of all fat
¼ cup (½ stick) unsalted butter
½ cup minced shallots
2 teaspoons Dijon-style mustard
1 cup fine fresh bread crumbs
¼ teaspoon dried thyme, crumbled
1 tablespoon minced fresh rosemary leaves
salt and pepper
⅓ cup minced fresh parsley leaves

1) Preheat oven to 450°F. Bring lamb to room temperature.

2) Heat the butter and sauté the shallots for 2 minutes and remove from the heat. Let cool. Add mustard. In a shallow bowl, combine the thyme, the breadcrumbs, the rosemary, salt and pepper to taste and mix well. Stir in the parsley. Salt and pepper the lamb, dip in butter-and-mustard mixture, then spread the crumb mixture evenly over the racks of lamb.

3) In a roasting pan, arrange the lamb, resting on the bones with the meat side up. Roast for 30 minutes or until a meat thermometer registers 130 to 135°F for medium-rare meat.

4) Transfer the lamb carefully to a work surface and let it stand 10 minutes. Slice between the ribs and serve 4 rib chops per person. ✒

Rosemary Rack of Lamb

Since I am of Italian descent , when I hear people speak of "southern country cooking," I usually think of Sicilian recipes. However that wasn't the case when I received a call from producer John Scura at the Vicki show asking if I'd prepare a southern country buffet to complement the appearance of two southern ladies who were guests on the show. As it turned out the guests were indeed southern – USA style! Dixie Carter, star of the hit TV series Designing Women, along with etiquette expert, columnist and author Marjabelle Stewart and Vicki (who's southern, too, in a sense . . . she's from southern California) starred that day. Marjabelle demonstrated the proper way to serve yourself and guests from a country plantation buffet luncheon. How to hold your glass with a napkin in one hand (so you can shake hands with the other). Even instructions on the proper way to use your napkin (the crease should be facing you). I have modified the following spareribs recipe provided by Marjabelle and have used it on several occasions. This is really two recipes in one: my favorite barbecue sauce (which also works well with pre-roasted beef ribs) and the process for cooking ribs. It's important not to baste too early with barbecue sauces, as the spices will become bitter. Generally speaking, ribs take 40-45 minutes to cook over charcoals. Make sure to baste with barbecue sauce during the last 25 minutes of cooking. P.S. although barbecued ribs are big with cowboys, this is pronounced "row-day-o" . . . as in Beverly Hills!

98

RODEO DRIVE SPARERIBS
Serves 4

1 tablespoon butter
¼ cup chopped onion
½ cup water
2 tablespoons vinegar
1 tablespoon Worcestershire sauce
¼ cup lemon juice
2 or 3 dashes of Tabasco sauce, according to taste
2 tablespoons brown sugar
1 cup bottled chili sauce
½ teaspoon salt
½ teaspoon paprika
½ teaspoon pepper
1 teaspoon chili powder
1 teaspoon celery seed
4 pounds spareribs, parboiled (2 full sides of pork ribs)
1 large onion, thinly sliced
1 lemon, thinly sliced

1) In a saucepan large enough to hold the first 14 ingredients, heat the butter, sauté the chopped onion until golden brown and add the 12 ingredients. Allow the mixture to simmer 20 to 30 minutes.

2) After you've parboiled the ribs (placed in boiling water for 5 to 10 minutes), place the ribs, rounded side down, over hot coals and grill 10 minutes on each side. Then, brush occasionally with the sauce, turn the ribs, and cook 10 minutes more.

3) Place onion and lemon slices on the ribs and secure with toothpicks. Continue grilling without turning, brushing frequently with the barbecue sauce 25 to 30 minutes or until done. (To test, cut the meat between the bones. If it's no longer pink and pulls easily from the bone, the ribs are cooked.) Cut into portions with scissors and serve immediately. ✐

STEAK au POIVRE
Serves 2

2¾-inch-thick New York or Spencer steaks
1½ tablespoons black peppercorns, or to taste
¼ cup brandy
½ cup heavy cream
1 cup canned beef broth
salt
watercress for garnish

1) Trim excess fat from steaks; reserve a piece.

2) With the flat of a cleaver or meat pounder, coarsely crush the peppercorns between 2 sheets of waxed paper.

3) Press the crushed peppercorns into both sides of the steaks and flatten the steaks between sheets of waxed paper to ½-inch thickness.

4) Rub the reserved fat onto a skillet just large enough to hold the steaks. Over moderately high heat, sear the steaks for 1½ minutes on each side. Reduce heat to medium and cook the steaks for 1 to 2 minutes for rare meat and transfer to a heated platter.

5) Pour out any fat from the pan, and add the brandy to the pan and ignite it. Shake the pan until the flames burn out. Add the broth, the heavy cream and reduce the liquid over high heat by ½. Add salt to taste, pour sauce over the steaks and serve garnished with watercress. ✐

GRAND FINALES!

c h a p t e r 5

desserts

My dictionary defines a grand finale as a "stunning conclusion." That's what a good dessert is. It can be as lavish as a Busby Berkeley number, such as Flambé Berries, or as understated as Bogie's "Here's lookin' at you kid" from *Casablanca*, like Green Grapes in a Crème Fraîche. Grandiose or sublimely simple, a good dessert is like the farewell kiss after a romantic interlude: It summarizes everything about the evening and says "until the next time."

Sweets seem to be the common theme of today's desserts. Although the English serve fruit and nuts and the French favor fruit with cheese, here in the States dessert means *sweets*. There are a gazillion cookbooks dedicated to every type of dessert imaginable as well as an abundance of low fat, low sugar offerings. My rule of thumb is to make the desserts for parties of under thirty guests. Otherwise, I prefer to defer to the best pasty chef or bakery I know. They're the experts and have an artistry all their own.

The beauty of the following desserts is that most can be prepared in advance and require little attention prior to serving. Many store well and last for days.

Because the dessert is the last element of your meal, elegant presentation is essential. Adorning your offering with a silver serving piece, an elegant doily, a slice of fruit, a sprig of mint, or a leaf from your garden will make it all the more appealing and memorable.

It's popular at Hollywood parties to serve a composition of a number of desserts on the same plate. Two, three, or even four small portions of sweets are presented in a way that complements not just the meal itself, but also each other. For instance, try combining a Hand-Painted Sugar Cookie, a Classic Fudge Brownie, a Strawberry Shortcake and a dollop of Mango-Lime Mousse. You'll satisfy the sweet tooth of just about everyone – cookie fans, chocoholics, fruit lovers. Plus, the overall effect is beautiful. Be sure to design and compose the dessert elements on the plate before presenting this grand finale to each guest.

Chapter Five

Tea for Two

I had been conducting group cooking classes for Carrie Fisher at her home right up until she gave birth to daughter Billie. Frequently there, I'd had an eyeful of the gorgeous baby shower gifts received from family and friends. The house was raining ribbons! (No wonder they call it a "shower.") There seemed to be no end to the doorbell ringing, heralding new boxes arriving from specialty boutiques around the country and the best of Beverly Hills. What could I possibly give her that she didn't already have?

After much thought, I decided to give her my *time*. Recalling when my son was born, I figured the best thing a new mother could have was lunch and dinner prepared for three whole days. So . . . I was hers!

One afternoon I arrived at Carrie's to prepare dinner. After gently shouting a "Hello-Hello" while letting myself in, Carrie's elated voice from upstairs announced my presence to someone downstairs. Carrie then explained that I was the man who had given himself to her. Much to my embarrassment, Carrie asked this "someone" if she had ever had such a gift.

Delighted at her euphoria (every sleep-deprived mother should be so happy), I was curious about the unseen person and cautiously glanced down the hallway. In the living room, surrounded in shadow was the silhouette of a strikingly beautiful woman. It was impossible to determine her likeness, but it was clear that she was elegantly poised.

Carrie continued speaking from upstairs, asking if I had met Betty.

Betty, I thought, who is Betty? My mind was a whirring Rolodex. Betty Ford . . . Big Betty Boop . . . Betty Crocker . . . Bette Davis . . . Betty who?

Just then, out from the shadow effortlessly emerged the luminous Lauren Bacall, known to her friends as Betty, still stunning and as sultry as when she made her screen debut in *To Have and Have Not*. I was face to face with a legend. Suddenly my favorite films came to mind: *The Big Sleep*, written by William Faulkner and based on Raymond Chandler's complex mystery; *How to Marry a Millionaire* with Marilyn Monroe and Betty Grable, and so many other classics. I had enjoyed her performance in the Broadway musical "Applause" from the balcony. Now, here she was, live at Carrie's. What could be better than this?

Graciously, she extended her hand and said hello. Moments later, Carrie came downstairs and we decided to have tea. What a grand idea I thought, before it hit me that I had come to prepare dinner. Tea? Who was prepared for tea? Not *moi*!

Frantically I searched through Carrie's pantry. What to serve? Fortunately, Carrie was well supplied with tea. But what else? Finally I discovered some wafer cookies that I elegantly displayed on a plate (never underestimate eye appeal) and I found some leftover brownies I had made. Now don't laugh. There's a lot to be said for leftovers. Especially good ones. Not too sweet, these Classic Fudge Brownies stay deliciously moist when stored in an airtight container. This "leftover" tea was a hit.

CLASSIC FUDGE BROWNIES
Makes 16

3 ounces unsweetened chocolate,
   coarsely chopped
½ cup (1 stick) unsalted butter, cut into bits
¾ cup sifted all-purpose flour
½ teaspoon double-acting baking powder
pinch of salt
2 large eggs
1¼ cups sugar
1 teaspoon vanilla
1 cup chopped walnuts

1) Preheat oven to 350°F. Butter and flour an 8-inch square baking pan. (If you don't want the "white flour" look, dust the pan with unsweetened cocoa, or use a nonstick spray.)

2) In a heavy saucepan, melt the chocolate and butter over low heat, stirring until smooth and let the mixture cool completely.

2) Into a bowl, sift together the flour, baking powder and salt.

3) In the large bowl of an electric mixer, beat the eggs, add the sugar a little at a time while beating and beat the mixture at high speed for 3 minutes or until thick and pale. Stir in the chocolate mixture and vanilla, add the flour mixture, stirring until well blended and stir in the walnuts.

4) Pour batter into the baking pan, smoothing the top and bake it in the middle of the oven for 25-30 minutes, or until it pulls away slightly from the sides of the pan and a cake tester inserted in the center comes out with crumbs adhering to it. Let brownies cool completely in the pan before cutting them into squares. ✒

These cookies have a very folksy charm. Using the basic food colorings, you can create almost any color imaginable.

HAND-PAINTED SUGAR COOKIES
Makes about 4 dozen

½ cup (1 stick) butter, softened
1 cup granulated sugar
1 egg
1 tablespoon cream
½ teaspoon vanilla or almond extract
2 cups all-purpose flour
¼ teaspoon salt
1 teaspoon baking powder
Cookie Paint

1) Preheat oven to 375°F. Cream the butter and add sugar gradually, beating until fluffy. Add the egg, cream and vanilla, beating well after each addition.

2) In a separate bowl, sift dry ingredients together and add to the butter mixture. Mix well. Form into 2 or 3 balls and chill for 1 hour.

3) On a lightly floured surface, roll ½ or ⅓ of the dough, keeping the rest in the refrigerator. For crisp cookies, roll paper-thin. For softer cookies, roll ⅛- to ¼-inch thick.

4) With a cookie cutter, cut into desired shapes, keeping cuttings close together. With a spatula, transfer cookies to lightly greased cookie sheet placing ½-inch apart. Paint as desired. Bake cookies 6 to 8 minutes until set, but not brown. Remove with spatula to waxed paper. Allow to cool completely before storing in an airtight container.

Cookie Paint

1 egg yolk
¼ teaspoon water
liquid (not gel) food coloring

With a fork, mix together the egg and water and remove any lumps. Divide into 3 or 4 small custard cups or aluminum mini-muffin tins. Add 1 or 2 drops of food coloring to each cup and stir thoroughly. Using new watercolor brushes, test each color (using a separate brush, or rinsing thoroughly each time) on a paper towel first to ensure you've achieved the desired hue. Dip brush into paint and decorate as desired. If egg yolk paint thickens, add a drop of water. Paint can be stored for several days by covering muffin tin "palette" with foil.

Food coloring comes in many colors. If you just have the basics, here are some combinations:
yellow + red = orange   yellow + blue = green
red + blue = purple   orange + blue = brown ✐

CHOCOLATE-DIPPED COCONUT MACAROONS
Makes about 2½ dozen

4 large egg whites
1⅓ cups sugar
8 ounces of fine quality bittersweet chocolate, chopped
½ teaspoon salt
1½ teaspoons vanilla
2½ cups sweetened flaked coconut
¼ cup plus 2 tablespoons all-purpose flour

1) Preheat oven to 300°F. In a heavy-bottomed saucepan, stir together the egg whites, sugar, salt, vanilla and coconut. Sift in the flour and stir the mixture until well combined.

2) Cook the mixture over moderate heat for 5 minutes, stirring constantly. Increase the heat to high and continue stirring and cooking the mixture for 3 to 5 minutes more, or until it thickens and begins to pull away from the sides of the pan. Transfer the mixture to a bowl and let it cool slightly. Cover the surface of the mixture with plastic wrap and chill until just cold.

3) Drop heaping teaspoons of the mixture 2 inches apart onto a buttered baking sheet and bake in batches in the middle of the oven for 20 to 25 minutes until pale golden. Transfer to a rack and let cool.

4) In a small metal bowl set over barely simmering water, melt the chocolate, stirring until smooth. Remove the bowl from the heat and dip the macaroons 1 at a time into the chocolate, coating them halfway, allowing the excess chocolate to drip off. As they are dipped, transfer the macaroons onto a foiled-lined tray. Before serving, chill uncovered for 30 minutes to 1 hour or until chocolate is set.

5) Cookies can be stored in an airtight container separated by layers of waxed paper for up to 4 days. Let stand 20 minutes before serving. Do not freeze. ✐

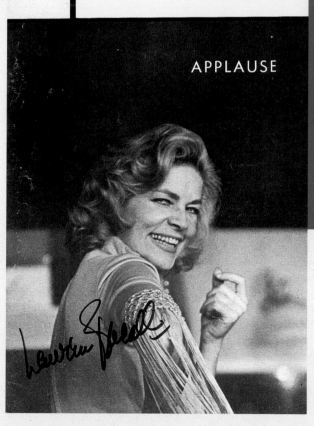

This is one of my mother's staples. She would always refer to them as her "Greek cookies" since the recipe came from our neighbors who emigrated from Athens. I can't remember a day when we didn't have these cookies that Mom lovingly wrapped in waxed paper and stored in shoe boxes. When I started catering, this was one of the first recipes I asked her to send from Chicago. Make sure the cookies are hot when you dip them into the powdered sugar or else it won't adhere.

MOM'S GREEK BUTTER COOKIES
Makes about 1 ½ dozen

1 cup (2 sticks) unsalted butter, softened
3 egg yolks
½ cup honey
1 cup canola oil
1 tablespoon vanilla
5 cups flour
1½ teaspoons double-acting baking powder
1½ teaspoons baking soda
¼ teaspoon salt
powdered sugar for dusting

1) Preheat oven to 375°F. In the large bowl of electric mixer, cream together the butter and honey. Slowly add the oil until the mixture is light and creamy in texture. Add 1 egg yolk at a time, mixing to incorporate. Add the vanilla.

2) Into a bowl, sift together the flour, baking soda, baking powder and salt. Stir this mixture into the butter-honey mixture. Mix long enough to form a dough. Don't overmix.

3) Lightly butter the baking sheets. Fill a teaspoon with dough and transfer to the pan, using your hands to keep the dough in an oval.

Use the back of the spoon to lightly press down the top of the cookie. Bake 15 minutes or until lightly golden.

4) Remove the pan from the oven and using a tong, immediately dip each cookie into powdered sugar and transfer to waxed paper to cool. Store in an airtight container at room temperature. ✒

These are featured in my annual Christmas gift baskets. They are easy to prepare if you can purchase the necessary orange oil at specialty stores such as Williams-Sonoma. To get extra fancy, try coating half the cookie with melted chocolate before serving. Italians traditionally dunk their biscotti in wine while Americans are fond of them with coffee.

WALNUT-ORANGE BISCOTTI
Makes 6 dozen

3⅔ cups all-purpose flour
2 cups walnut pieces
1 teaspoon double-action baking powder
¼ teaspoon baking soda
3 large eggs
1⅓ cups sugar
2½ tablespoons zest from 1 large lemon
2½ tablespoons zest from 1 large orange
1 teaspoon pure orange oil
½ cup (1 stick) unsalted butter, melted

1) Preheat the oven to 350°F. Line a sheet pan with parchment paper cut to fit the bottom.

2) Blend the flour, walnuts, baking powder and baking soda in a large bowl until the nuts are evenly mixed.

3) In a 3-quart mixing bowl, break 2 of the eggs, separate the third egg and drop the yolk into the bowl. Reserve the white separately. Whisk the eggs, adding the sugar, the zests and the orange oil. Slowly whisk in the melted butter and when it is well blended, pour it into the bowl with the flour mixture.

4) Mix and fold all ingredients together (except for the egg white) until the liquid is absorbed and all ingredients are incorporated.

5) On a lightly floured work surface, knead and squeeze the dough into a stiff mass.

6) Divide the dough in half and press each half into a log 14 inches long. Press the ends in as you roll to keep it neat. Lift each log as shaped onto the parchment pan, press the top to flatten it slightly. The logs should be oval. Beat the reserved egg white with a fork until smooth and brush it lightly over the tops.

7) Bake in the oven until the logs are light brown but still give slightly when pressed, about 30 minutes. Remove the pan from the oven, reduce the oven temperature to 350°F. Let the logs cool on the pan for 15 minutes.

8) One at a time, remove the logs to a cutting board and cut on the diagonal into ½-inch pieces in traditional biscotti style. Lay the slices on their side and return the sheet to the oven. Bake the biscotti about 15 minutes until they are light brown. Put them on a wire rack and when they are thoroughly cool, store in an airtight container. They will keep for weeks. ✒

Walnut-Orange **Biscotti**

Chocolate-Dipped **& Coconut Macaroons**

Queen Victoria would turn over in her grave at the thought of having a tea party without scones. This English tea staple is served with clotted cream, Devonshire cream (American whipped cream) jams, marmalade and lemon curd – actually it's great with any sweet spread!

GINGER SCONES

Makes 2 dozen

2 cups all-purpose flour
3 tablespoons sugar plus 2 tablespoons for
   sprinkling the scones
2 teaspoons double-acting baking powder
½ teaspoon baking soda
1 teaspoon cinnamon
½ teaspoon salt
2½ teaspoon ground ginger
5½ tablespoons cold unsalted butter, cut into
   ½-inch pieces
1 large egg
¼ cup unsulfured molasses
½ cup buttermilk
2 tablespoons milk plus additional for brushing
   the scones
⅓ cup finely chopped crystallized ginger

1) Preheat the oven to 350°F. Sift together the flour, sugar, baking powder, baking soda, cinnamon, salt, and ground ginger. Add the butter and combine the mixture until it resembles coarse meal.

2) In a separate bowl, whisk the egg with the molasses, buttermilk, 2 tablespoons milk, the

remaining 2 tablespoons sugar and the crystallized ginger. Add the egg mixture to the flour mixture, stirring with a fork until it just forms a sticky yet manageable dough. Knead the dough gently on a floured surface, pat it out into a 1-inch-thick round.

3) With a 2-inch biscuit cutter dipped in flour, or a 2-inch-diameter glass dipped in flour, cut out as many rounds as possible and transfer them to a lightly greased baking sheet. Gather the remaining scraps, pat out the dough and cut more rounds.

4) Brush the rounds with additional milk, sprinkle with additional sugar and bake in batches in the middle of the oven 10 to 15 minutes or until golden. ✓

LEMON-THYME THINS

Makes 5 dozen

3¼ cups all-purpose flour
2 teaspoons baking soda
½ teaspoon salt
3 teaspoons finely chopped lemon-thyme leaves
1 cup (2 sticks) unsalted butter, softened
1½ cups sugar
2½ tablespoons lemon zest
1 large egg
3 tablespoons lemon juice
¾ tablespoon finely grated gingerroot
powdered sugar

1) If baking cookies immediately, preheat oven to 350°F. Sift together flour, baking soda, and salt. Stir in thyme.

2) Using an electric mixer, beat butter, sugar and zest until fluffy. Combine with flour mixture.

3) Divide the dough in half and form each half into a roll about 14 by 1½-inches. Wrap each roll in wax paper and foil and freeze for at least 20 minutes. (Or up to 3 weeks. If the roll is frozen through, bring to room temperature before slicing.)

4) Slice roll diagonally in ¼-inch thick ovals, and cut each oval in half. Bake on ungreased cookie sheets spaced 1½ inch apart in upper and lower thirds of oven. After 6 minutes, switch the positions of the pans. After 6 more minutes, remove the cookies with spatula to racks to cool. Dust with powdered sugar. ✓

To prevent apples, pears, avocados, and other fruits and vegetables from discoloring while left sitting during preparation, dip them or brush them with the juice of a lemon.

Tea for Two Thousand

Patrick Swayze (better known as "Buddy" to his friends) and I met in Los Angeles after he and his wife Lisa moved here from New York. In the Big Apple he had danced in the Broadway musical *Grease*. But old Texas high school football injuries made dancing difficult, so he and Lisa, who's a wonderful dancer, too, relocated to L.A. to try the big screen.

Buddy and I became friends while doing scenes together in Milton Katselas's acting class. At this time Buddy and Lisa lived in a fourplex in what's known as the Miracle Mile district. There were no "miracles" happening at this time, however. In fact, one day Buddy confided they were so broke they were living off oranges from a neighbor's tree.

My catering business had been going awhile and I always had food in the fridge. Happy to share, I insisted they come over. They did many, many times and I have fond memories of the dinner conversations shared in my kitchen, as well as Thanksgiving, New Year's Eve, and a spectacular motorcycle camping trip to Big Sur. I've been cooking for and with them for years, and now, I'm happy to say, it's all being enjoyed under much better circumstances.

What I like and admire most about Buddy is that he's one of those guys who's into mastering whatever he sets out to do, whether it is skydiving, calf-roping or acting. (Who didn't love *Dirty*

The first thing I did when I got to Albuquerque was to go on a tasting spree to find the very best baked goods. I was delighted (and relieved) to discover Le Chantilly, where I ordered many of the goodies served. If you live in Albuquerque, forget about making this recipe. Just go over to 8216 Menaul N.E. at the Hoffman Town Shopping Center and buy the squares! Otherwise, follow my recipe below. Done in two steps so the crust has its own distinct flavor, it's a little time-consuming, but well worth the extra effort.

CITRUS SQUARES
Makes 16

1 cup sifted all-purpose flour
¼ cup sifted powdered sugar
½ teaspoon grated lemon rind
½ cup (1 stick) cold unsalted butter,
   cut into bits
2 large eggs
1 cup granulated sugar
6 tablespoons fresh lemon juice
2 tablespoons all-purpose flour
½ teaspoon double-acting baking powder
powdered sugar for garnish

1) Preheat oven to 375°F. Combine the flour (except for 2 tablespoons), powdered sugar and lemon rind.

2) Cut in the butter until the mixture resembles coarse meal. Press the mixture evenly into the bottom of an 8-inch square ungreased baking pan.

3) Place the pan on a baking sheet and bake the pastry base in the lower third of the oven for 18 to 20 minutes, or until golden around the edges. (The base will be only partially baked at this point.)

4) In the large bowl of an electric mixer, combine the eggs and the sugar. Add the lemon juice and beat the mixture for 5 minutes, or until pale and smooth. Combine the flour and baking powder. Whisk the flour mixture into the egg mixture and combine well.

5) Pour the filling mixture over the partially baked base and continue baking the dessert in the pan on the baking sheet for 25 minutes. Sift powdered sugar over the dessert and let cool on a rack. Cut into 2-inch squares.

Store in an airtight container but do not refrigerate or the base will become soggy. ✓

Dancing or *Ghost*?) Fortunately for me, he's never taken up catering. Otherwise, I never would have received the call from Lisa a while back for what is perhaps my most unusual job ever.

Lisa explained that she and Buddy, who are avid horse lovers, had purchased an Arabian mare named Tammen who would be appearing at the National Arabian Horse Show in Albuquerque, New Mexico. In the horse world, it's a tradition for the owners of a new horse to host an "introductory" party at the stables for three to four hundred people. But for this occasion, Buddy and Lisa had something slightly larger in mind.

So, off I went to Albuquerque to survey the site of what would be the biggest tea party this mad hatter had ever seen. The reception was to be held at the fairgrounds youth center and I remember being confounded trying to configure the best serving arrangements for what I anticipated to be a crowd of maybe five hundred people.

The day of the party, while thumbing through the horse show program, I came across a full page ad inviting *everyone* to attend Tammen's Tea Party. I had figured five hundred. But glancing at the grandstands, it seemed like thousands was a more likely count. No sooner did I start tallying food quantities than my assistant excitedly announced he'd heard a local radio DJ announce the party on the air! I frantically checked my figures again. Would there be enough? How many people actually did listen to that radio station?

COCONUT ANGEL FOOD CAKE with ORANGE FROSTING
Serves 8-10

Cake

8 egg whites at room temperature
½ teaspoon salt
½ teaspoon cream of tartar
1 cup superfine granulated sugar
½ teaspoon almond extract
½ teaspoon vanilla
¾ cup cake flour
1 ½ cups shredded unsweetened coconut

1) Preheat oven to 275°F. Beat egg whites with salt until frothy. Add salt and cream of tartar and continue beating whites until they hold soft peaks. Sprinkle ½ cup superfine sugar over the whites, 2 tablespoons at a time and continue beating until peaks are stiff. With a rubber spatula fold in the remaining ½ cup superfine sugar, 2 tablespoons at a time, the almond extract and vanilla.

2) Sift the cake flour 4 times onto a sheet of waxed paper. Sift it over the egg whites, ¼ at a time, folding it lightly into the whites. Fold in ½ cup of the coconut. Pour the batter into an ungreased 9-inch tube pan and bake the cake in the middle of the oven for 1 ½ hours. Remove cake from oven, suspend it upside down on the neck of a bottle and let it hang for 1 ½ to 2 hours, or until cooled completely.

Orange Frosting

1¼ cups granulated sugar
2 egg whites
¼ cup fresh orange juice
1 tablespoon light corn syrup
1 teaspoon grated orange rind
pinch of salt

1) Increase oven temperature to 350°F. Toast the remaining 1 cup coconut in a baking pan in the middle of the oven for 10 minutes, shaking the pan occasionally. Let coconut cool.

2) In a separate bowl, combine the granulated sugar, egg whites, orange juice, corn syrup, grated orange rind and salt. Set the bowl over a saucepan containing 3 inches of boiling water and whisk the mixture until it is hot and foamy. Return the bowl to the mixer and beat the frosting at high speed for 7 minutes or until it is cool and holds stiff peaks. Makes about 3 cups.

3) With a sharp knife, release the cake from the sides and center tube of the pan and invert onto a rack. Place a cake plate on top of the cake. Turn cake right side up and frost. Press the toasted coconut onto the sides of the cake. ✧

I love pumpkin pie and the spicier the better. I usually serve it in the fall during holiday time and can't imagine a Thanksgiving or Christmas without one. This recipe has the best blend of spices and always turns out well.

PUMPKIN PIE
Makes 1 9-inch pie

1½ cups canned pumpkin puree
1 cup half-and-half
3 large eggs
⅓ cup firmly packed light brown sugar
⅓ cup sugar
1 teaspoon cinnamon
1 teaspoon vanilla
½ teaspoon ground ginger
½ teaspoon salt
¼ teaspoon freshly grated nutmeg
a pinch of ground cloves
whipped cream
½ Pie Crust recipe (recipe follows)

1) On a floured surface, roll out the dough to ⅛-inch and fit it into a 9-inch pie pan. Crimp the edges decoratively and chill uncovered for 1 hour.

2) Preheat the oven to 425°F.

3) In a large bowl, combine all the above ingredients, except the whipped cream, until smooth. Pour the mixture into the pie shell. Bake the pie on a baking sheet in the lower ⅓ of the oven for 15 minutes. Reduce the heat to 350°F. Bake for 30 to 35 minutes more until a toothpick inserted in the center comes out clean. Let pie cool before serving with whipped cream. ✧

109

Much to my delight, with a few resourceful "Nick's Tricks," there was enough of everything to please the enormous turnout! Over 2,500 people, including screaming fans, "the horsey set" and country music star Larry Gatlin had tea at the fairgrounds that afternoon. And believe it or not . . . Tammen did too! ✧

I was a well-established caterer before I learned to make pie crust. For some reason, it always frightened me. A dear lady by the name of Josephine spent hours with me making pie crusts until I got the knack. Here's the recipe, which you can master too. However, if you're like I used to be and afraid of pie crusts, Pillsbury makes an excellent ready-to-bake pie crust found in the refrigerated section of the market. All you do is bring it to room temperature, unfold it and place it on a pie pan, pierce it with a fork, cover with a piece of waxed paper or parchment, weight it with dried beans (or use the small, clean round pebbles as in France) to ensure it bakes evenly and place in the oven. Just before it's completely golden, remove beans or pebbles or paper, and return to oven and continue baking until golden brown.

PIE CRUST
Makes 2 single-crust 9-inch pies

2 cups all-purpose flour
1 tablespoon salt
2 tablespoons sugar
2 tablespoons chilled unsalted butter
⅔ cup chilled vegetable shortening
scant ½ cup ice water

1) Sift together the flour, salt and sugar.

2) Cut the butter and shortening into the flour mixture with a pastry blender until it resembles pea size. Sprinkle the dough with ½ the water and blend the dough until the water is incorporated. Form the dough into a ball, knead lightly with the heel of your hand against a smooth surface for a few seconds to distribute the fat evenly and re-form into a ball. Add more water if needed.

3) Dust the dough with flour, wrap in waxed paper and chill for 1 hour.

4) Divide the dough in half and on a lightly floured, cool surface, roll out to a desired thickness.

5) Place on pie pan and bake as noted above.

The secret to making great pie dough is to work quickly before the ingredients warm. Keep the shortening ice cold and keep an ice cube in the water.

Three things are essential to this recipe's success: A food grinder (a food processor won't give the desired consistency), a week's time, and an affinity for handling pie dough. With those, you'll find this pie superior to the traditional mincemeat pie.

PEAR MINCEMEAT PIE
Makes 1 9-inch pie

6 firm Anjou or Bartlett pears
juice from 1 lemon
1 orange, quartered, seeded but unpeeled
1 cup sugar
½ cup golden raisins
¼ cup minced crystallized ginger
¾ teaspoon ground mace
¾ teaspoon ground allspice
¾ teaspoon cinnamon
1½ cups chopped walnuts
¼ cup brandy
1 egg white, lightly beaten
½ Pie Crust recipe

1) Peel, core and quarter the pears. Put them in a bowl of water with the lemon juice. Drain the pears and put them and the orange through the coarse blade of a food grinder into a mixing bowl.

2) In a heavy skillet, add the pear mixture, sugar, raisins, ginger and all the spices. Bring it to a boil, stirring, and simmer for 1 ½ hours or until thick enough for a wooden spoon to stand in it.

3) Remove the skillet from the heat and stir in the walnuts and brandy. Cover and chill the mixture for at least 1 week.

4) Using two-thirds of the pie dough, roll it into ⅛-inch thickness and fit it into a 9-inch pie pan. Trim the excess, leaving 1-inch overhang. Brush the bottom and the sides with the egg white, cover and chill, with plastic wrap and chill for about 1 hour. Reserve remaining egg white.

5) Preheat oven and a baking sheet to 425°F. Gather up the dough scraps, add to remaining dough and roll into a rectangle which is ¼-inch thick, 7 inches wide and 12 inches long. Cut out fourteen ½-inch-wide strips with a pastry wheel. Put the strips on a floured baking sheet and chill them for 10 minutes or until firm.

6) Fill the pie shell with the mincemeat and moisten the edge of the dough with water. Arrange the strips in a lattice pattern over the top. Press the lattice ends into the pie shell and trim the excess. Crimp the edges decoratively.

7) Place the pie pan on a baking sheet in the lower third of the oven, and bake for 20 minutes, brushing it twice with the reserved egg white for 20 minutes. Reduce the heat to 350°F and bake 30 minutes more. Serve warm. ✐

PECAN PIE
Makes an 11½" pie

2 cups dark corn syrup
1 cup sugar
3 tablespoons unsalted butter, melted
3 tablespoons all-purpose flour
5 large eggs
1 tablespoon dark rum
½ teaspoon vanilla
2 cups pecan halves
whipped cream or vanilla ice cream
¾ Pie Crust recipe (pg. 110) substituting sugar for salt in the recipe

1) Preheat the oven to 400°F. Prepare the pie crust dough and roll it out to ⅛-inch thickness. Transfer it to an 11½-inch pie plate. Trim the excess dough from the sides of the pie shell, leaving a 1-inch overhang. Fold the overhang over the rim, pressing it onto the sides of the shell, forming a decorative edge. Pierce the bottom of the shell with a fork and chill for 30 minutes.

2) Line the pie shell with waxed paper weighted with dried beans or rice and bake in the lower third of the oven for 15 minutes. Remove the waxed paper and the beans or rice and bake the shell for another 10 minutes, or until lightly golden. Let the pie shell cool on a rack.

3) Reduce the oven temperature to 375°F. In a large bowl, combine the dark corn syrup, sugar, melted butter and flour. In another bowl, lightly beat the eggs with the rum and vanilla. Add the egg mixture to the sugar mixture and combine well.

4) Arrange the pecans in the pastry shell and pour the filling in slowly. Bake the pie in the middle of the oven for 40 minutes or until it is set. Let the pie cool on a rack. Serve slightly warm, accompanied by the whipped cream or ice cream. ✐

CARROT CAKE with CREAM CHEESE FROSTING
Serves 8-10

Cake

2 cups all-purpose flour
2 cups granulated sugar
2 teaspoons baking soda
1 teaspoon salt
1 tablespoon cinnamon
pinch of allspice
4 large eggs
1 cup vegetable oil
4 cups finely grated carrots (about 1 pound)

1) Preheat oven to 350°F. Line 3 8-inch round cake pans with wax paper and butter the paper. Dust pans with flour and remove the excess.

2) Into a bowl, sift together the flour, granulated sugar, baking soda, salt, cinnamon and allspice. In a separate large bowl, beat the eggs for 1 minute or until frothy, and beat in the oil while pouring it into the bowl in a slow stream. Gradually beat in the flour mixture and continue beating the batter until it is just smooth. Stir in the carrots.

3) Divide the batter among the cake pans, smoothing the tops, and bake the layers in the middle of the oven for 25 to 30 minutes, or until a cake tester inserted in the centers comes out clean. Let the layers cool in the pans on racks for 10 minutes. Run a thin knife around the edges of the cake pans and invert the layers onto racks. Let them cool completely and peel off the waxed paper.

Frosting

1 pound cream cheese, softened
1 stick (½ cup) unsalted butter, softened
4 cups powdered sugar
2 teaspoons vanilla
½ cup apricot jam
violet candy flowers for garnish

1) In a large bowl cream together the cream cheese and the butter. Add the powdered sugar, a little at a time, beating while you add the vanilla.

2) Set 1 cake layer on a serving plate, spread ¼ the apricot jam over it and top it with another cake layer. Spread the layer with remaining jam and top it with the remaining cake layer. Spread the frosting over the sides and top of the cake and garnish with violet candy flowers. ✐

Strawberry Shortcake

Nothing heralds summer louder than fresh strawberries. One of my favorite ways to serve them is the traditional Strawberry Shortcake. Nothing is easier to prepare – especially when the berries are so readily available.

STRAWBERRY SHORTCAKE
Serves 8

3 pints ripe strawberries, hulled
½ cup plus 2 tablespoons sugar
¼ cup fresh lemon juice
2 cups all-purpose flour
1 tablespoon double-acting baking powder
¼ teaspoon salt
2 tablespoons unsalted butter, cut into bits and
   chilled, plus butter for spreading
1½ teaspoons minced lemon rind
¾ to 1 cup heavy cream
milk for brushing the biscuits
lightly whipped cream
8 small unhulled strawberries for garnish

1) Coarsely chop 1 pint of the strawberries.

2) In a heavy-bottomed stainless steel saucepan, combine the chopped strawberries with ½ cup sugar and ¼ cup lemon juice. Bring the liquid to a boil, cook over moderately high heat, stirring for 10 minutes until it is thickened and reduced to about 1 ¼ cups. Transfer the mixture to a bowl and let it cool.

3) Once the mixture has completely cooled, slice the remaining 2 pints of strawberries and add them to the mixture. Add lemon juice to taste and let the mixture stand for 1 hour.

4) Butter a baking sheet. Preheat oven to 400°F.

5) In a large bowl, sift the flour, the 2 tablespoons of sugar, baking powder and salt and cut in the 2 tablespoons of butter and lemon rind. Mix until it resembles coarse meal. Add enough heavy cream to make the dough soft.

6) Form the dough into a ball and pat it out to ½-inch thickness on a well-floured surface. Using a 4-inch-diameter glass or a biscuit cutter dipped in flour, cut out rounds and place on baking sheets 2 inches apart. Gather up the scraps and gently form into a ball and pat out and cut again until all the dough is used. Brush the tops lightly with the milk and bake for 15 to 20 minutes in the middle of the oven until they have risen and bronzed.

7) Split the biscuits with a fork while they are warm and spread with some of the remaining butter. Mound half of the biscuit with the strawberries and top it with the other biscuit half garnished with a dollop of whipped cream and a whole berry. ✎

KEY LIME PIE
Makes a 9-inch pie

4 egg yolks
1 can sweetened condensed milk
½ cup fresh lime juice
½ teaspoon cream of tartar
6 egg whites
¾ cup sugar
½ Pie Crust recipe (see page 110)

1) Preheat oven to 350°F. Beat the egg yolks until lemon colored. Slowly blend in condensed milk. Add lime juice and mix well.

2) For meringue, in a separate bowl add cream of tartar to egg whites and beat until foamy. Continue beating, adding sugar, 1 tablespoon at a time, until the egg whites form stiff peaks.

3) To the egg yolks, fold in 6 tablespoons of the meringue. Pour the filling into a 9-inch baked pie shell.

4) Top with remaining meringue and bake until golden brown. Let cool and serve. ✎

Nick's Tip!

Never wash strawberries before refrigerating: They will become mushy. Store in a colander or plastic woven basket so the air can circulate. Wash immediately prior to preparation or just before serving whole.

113

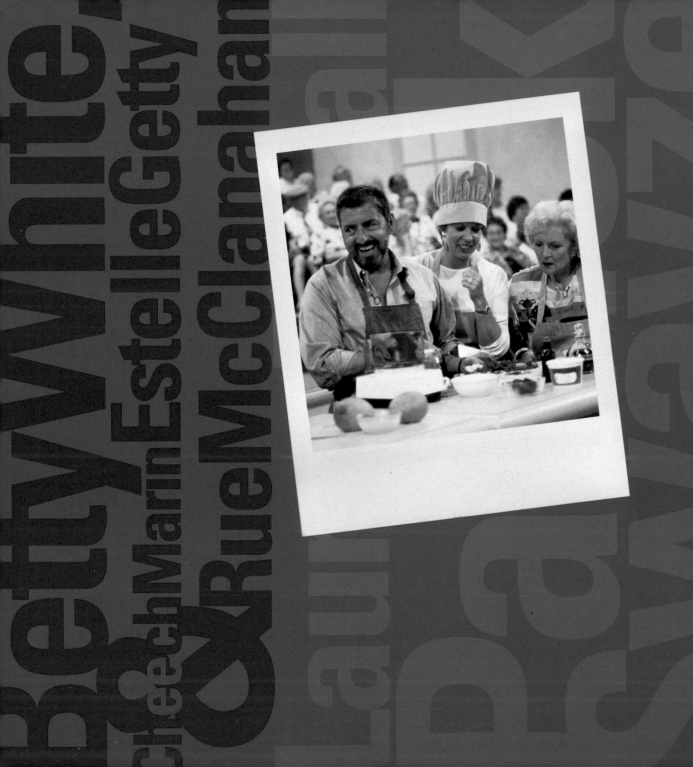

My Favorite Cheesecake

In 1992 I was asked to "cook something special" on one of the first episodes of a new TV series starring Vicki Lawrence. Featured on the *Vicki!* show would be the stars of the long running hit television series *The Golden Girls* who were now promoting a new series, *The Golden Palace*. On this show, Bea Arthur's character had married and moved away. Now the remaining "girls" had new careers. Arthur's feisty Italian mother Sophia (Estelle Getty), the nitwit Rose (Betty White) and the profusely passionate Blanche (Rue McClanahan) were operating a hotel called The Golden Palace. New to the series, playing the hotel cook, was comedian Cheech Marin. I hadn't seen Cheech in a very long time, having met him in the seventies when he was riding high as half of the hippie comedy team "Cheech & Chong." He was ecstatic at having landed this prime-time part.

After much thought, I decided to prepare the gang's favorite TV food – cheesecake, which on the series they enjoyed eating for any occasion. Whether sad or happy, the girls would ritually discuss things over a slice of cheesecake. Having recently discovered a new recipe that I thought was quite special, I was very pleased with the opportunity to present it on the show. What made this confection unusual was that it was a chocolate cheesecake with only 175 calories per slice, as opposed to a traditional one with 650 calories per slice. Another plus was that is was delicious and easy to prepare.

In the segment, everyone wore aprons and Vicki sported a white toque hat, the signature headgear of all respectable chefs. She introduced me as "Chef Extraordinaire to the Stars" and before I knew it, I was mixing the ingredients with the girls' help before the studio audience and several million viewers. Moments later, thanks to the magic of television (meaning I had baked several before the show started), I produced the finished cheesecake. The last remaining task was the garnish. I decided to personalize each slice with a fruit reflecting the stars' TV characters: For Betty – bananas; Rue – passionfruit, Estelle – Sicilian grapes; Vicki – star fruit of course, and as for Cheech . . . well I couldn't find *his* favorite, because it's still illegal!

Everyone seemed to truly enjoy the cheesecake, including members of the studio audience we shared it with. However, the best dessert would actually be served to me a few weeks later. I received a call from an excited producer informing me that the show had invited viewers to write in for the recipe. They had, and in record-breaking numbers for such a new series. Over four thousand requests arrived – far more than they had anticipated and the biggest response the show had ever received. I was thrilled and so were the producers. Best yet, I was invited back. ✒

CHOCOLATE CHEESECAKE
Serves 12

½ cup crushed chocolate wafers (about 7)
1 cup lowfat cottage cheese
1 8-ounce package light cream cheese
1 cup sugar
⅓ cup unsweetened cocoa powder
3 tablespoons raspberry liqueur
1 teaspoon vanilla
½ cup egg substitute
3 tablespoons miniature semisweet chocolate
  pieces
raspberries or other fresh fruit for garnish

1) Preheat oven to 300°F. Sprinkle wafer crumbs evenly in the bottom of an 8-inch springform pan.

2) In a food processor or blender, process cottage cheese until smooth. Add cream cheese, sugar, cocoa powder, liqueur and vanilla and process until combined. (Mixture will be thick; scrape the sides of the container, if necessary.)

3) Transfer to a large bowl and stir in egg substitute and chocolate.

4) Pour into the prepared pan and bake 45-50 minutes or until cheesecake appears nearly set when gently shaken. Cool on a wire rack for at least 10 minutes to prevent the cheesecake from cracking. Loosen sides of pan. Cool another 30 minutes and remove sides of pan. Cool completely, then cover and chill for several hours or overnight.

5) Garnish with raspberries or other fruit. ✒

This is a light and lovely dessert that complements the moussaka dish I teach in my cooking classes. Don't discount it as being too rich because of crème fraîche. If you're seriously counting fat grams, consider using one of the many nonfat sour creams that have fooled even me.

GREEN GRAPES in CRÈME FRAÎCHE
Serves 2

1 large cluster of seedless green grapes, washed
  and removed from stems
½ pint of Crème Fraîche
½ to ¾ cup dark brown sugar, packed
fresh mint leaves or orange slices for garnish

Crème Fraîche:

1 quart whole cream (whipping cream)
3 tablespoons buttermilk

To make the crème fraîche: In a nonmetallic bowl, mix the cream and the buttermilk. Cover, store at room temperature, or place near warm stove for 24 to 36 hours. Refrigerate. (Like fresh yogurt, this can be stored in the refrigerator for up to 2 weeks.)

1) In a 2-quart glass bowl, add the grapes, brown sugar and crème fraîche according to taste and toss. Refrigerate until ready to serve from bowl, or present individually in a fruit cup garnished with fresh mint leaves or orange slices.

This can be made earlier in the day and refrigerated until needed. Just before serving, freshen the grapes with an added 1 or 2 tablespoons of crème fraîche. ✒

115

Chocolate Cheesecake

This recipe is a challenge and not for the faint-hearted. Making caramel is tricky and takes practice. Hot caramel burns — so be careful in handling it, and for safety's sake, keep a bowl of ice water handy. If this warning hasn't scared you off, proceed to make what I consider to be French perfection.

APPLE TARTE TATIN
(UPSIDE-DOWN APPLE TART)
Makes a 9-inch tart

½ cup (1 stick) unsalted butter
6 large Macintosh apples, peeled, cored and
  thinly sliced
1½ cups sugar
½ teaspoon grated lemon rind
6 tablespoons water
2 pinches of cream of tartar
1 package puff pastry
lightly whipped cream

1) Preheat the oven to 425°F. In a large skillet, melt the butter. Add the apples, ½ cup sugar and the lemon rind and toss the apples until they are softened but still retain their shape. Transfer the mixture to a sheet pan and cool.

2) In a heavy skillet, cook ½ cup sugar, 3 tablespoons water and 1 pinch of the cream of tartar over moderately high heat, washing any sugar crystals clinging to the sides of the pan with a brush dipped in cold water until mixture is a golden caramel.

3) Pour the caramel into a 9-inch pie pan, tilting to ensure the caramel coats the bottom of the pan evenly. Let it stand.

4) Starting with the outer rim of the pan, arrange the apple slices in slightly overlapping concentric circles on the caramel. Reverse the direction of the slices for each circle, until the caramel is completely covered. Cover this layer with another layer of apple slices, arranging each circle in the opposite direction from the bottom layer. Fill the pan with the remaining apple slices, smoothing them out evenly.

5) On a floured surface, roll the puff pastry to ⅛-inch thickness. Using a 9-inch plate as a guide, cut out a round of pastry and lay it over the apples. Do not press the dough onto the sides of the pan.

6) Heat a cookie sheet in the oven until hot. Put the tarte pan on the baking sheet in the middle of the oven and bake for approximately 50 minutes or until the crust is golden. Cool the tarte on a rack for 30 minutes, allowing the apples to absorb the caramel, then invert the tarte onto a serving dish.

7) About 1 hour before serving, make a caramel from the remaining ½ cup sugar, 3 tablespoons water and 1 pinch of cream of tartar. Pour the caramel on top of the apples and with a metal spatula dipped in boiling water, spread it evenly in one direction. Serve with whipped cream, spiked if you like, with a dash of brandy or rum. ✐

I've received many compliments for this cobbler, but none more appreciated than a rave that came from Geena Davis who enjoyed it at a baby shower.

BLUEBERRY COBBLER
Serves 8

2 1-pint baskets of blueberries
½ cup sugar
2 tablespoons cornstarch
3 tablespoons butter, melted
1 tablespoon lemon juice
1 teaspoon grated lemon rind
⅛ teaspoon ground cloves
¾ cup unsifted flour
¾ teaspoon baking powder
¼ teaspoon salt
1 large egg
2 tablespoons milk

1) Preheat oven to 400°F. Grease an 8-inch round baking dish. In the dish, combine the berries, ¼ cup sugar, cornstarch, 1 tablespoon butter, lemon juice and rind and cloves.

2) In a separate small bowl, combine flour, remaining ¼ cup sugar, baking power and salt. Stir in the egg, milk and the remaining 2 tablespoons butter until a soft dough forms. Drop by tablespoonfuls onto blueberry mixture.

3) Bake cobbler 30 to 35 minutes or until topping is golden brown and filling bubbles. Great topped with ice cream. ✐

CHOCOLATE LAYER CAKE
Serves 8 to 10

10 tablespoons softened unsalted butter plus
   additional butter for the waxed paper
2 cups cake flour (not self-rising) plus additional
   flour for the paper
1½ cups sugar
1 cup buttermilk
½ cup water
4 ounces unsweetened chocolate, melted
3 large eggs, separated
1 teaspoon vanilla
½ teaspoon double-acting baking powder
1 teaspoon baking soda
½ teaspoon salt

1) Preheat oven to 350°F. Butter three 8-inch x
2-inch round cake pans and line them with
waxed paper. Butter and flour the paper,
knocking out any excess flour.

2) In the large bowl of an electric mixer, cream
together 10 tablespoons of butter and the sugar
until the mixture is light and fluffy. Beat in the
buttermilk, water, chocolate, egg yolks and the
vanilla. Into the bowl sift the flour, the baking
powder, baking soda and salt and stir the batter
until it is just combined.

3) In a bowl, and using clean beaters, beat the
egg whites until they hold stiff peaks and fold
them into the batter gently but thoroughly.

4) Divide the batter among the prepared cake
pans and bake in the middle of the preheated
oven for 25 minutes or until a tester comes out
clean. Cool in the pans on racks for about 15
minutes, then turn the cakes out of the pans onto
the racks to cool completely.

Frosting

4½ ounces unsweetened chocolate
¼ cup (½ stick) plus ½ tablespoon unsalted
butter
3 cups powdered sugar
½ teaspoon salt
½ cup milk
1½ teaspoons vanilla

1) In a metal bowl set over a pan of barely
simmering water, melt the chocolate and the
butter, stirring until the mixture is smooth. Stir in
the powdered sugar, salt, milk and the vanilla and
stir until the frosting is well combined.

2) Set the bowl in a large bowl of ice water and
beat the frosting until it is thick enough to spread.

3) On a plate, arrange 1 of the cake layers, flat
side up. Spread with some of the frosting, top
with a second layer and frost. Add third layer, flat
side up, and spread the top and sides of the cake
with the remaining frosting. Good luck, and
happy chocolate dreams. ✒

*This fruitcake is for non-fruitcake lovers who won't object
to waiting a week (instead of a month) before tasting.*

FRUITCAKE
Makes four 9½ x 5-inch loaves

2 cups (4 sticks) unsalted butter
2¼ cups firmly packed light brown sugar
1 cup honey
10 eggs
4 cups sifted flour
2 teaspoons cinnamon
2 teaspoons double-acting baking powder
1 teaspoon ground allspice
¾ teaspoon salt
3 pounds dried apricots, sliced
2 pounds pecan halves
1½ pounds pitted dates, sliced
1 pound golden raisins
1 cup apricot nectar
½ cup light cream
2 tablespoons lemon juice
1 cup brandy
¼ cup orange-flavored liqueur

1) Preheat oven to 250°F. In a large bowl, cream
together the butter, brown sugar and honey. Add
the eggs one at a time, beating well after each
addition.

2) In a large bowl, sift together the flour,
cinnamon, baking powder, allspice and salt. Add
half of the flour mixture to the sugar mixture.

3) Dredge sliced apricots, pecan halves, sliced
dates and raisins in the remaining flour mixture.

4) In another bowl, combine apricot nectar, light
cream, lemon juice and add to batter. Fold in the
dried apricot mixture. Pour the batter into four
buttered and floured 9½ x 5-inch loaf pans and
bake the cakes for 2½ to 3 hours or until a knife
inserted in the center comes out clean.

5) Place the cake pans on racks to cool.

6) Combine the brandy and the orange liqueur,
sprinkle each cake with one-fourth of the
mixture. Let the cake stand for at least 1 hour.
Remove the cakes from the pans, wrap tightly in
foil and chill them for a week. Serve at room
temperature. ✒

Memories

One night during a cooking class at Carrie Fisher's a few of us were busy preparing an almost authentic Mexican meal. I say "almost" because I had planned on making a Mexican flan, but it takes a very long time. So I decided on an Italian chocolate cream custard that nicely balanced the dinner, yet was fairly quick to make.

I was elbow-deep in tamales when the side door leading into the kitchen slowly opened. It was someone I hadn't seen in twenty years. I was the first one to greet her and she returned my salutations smiling a friendly "hello" in an unmistakable voice. I couldn't help noticing she looked exactly the same as when our sons had attended school together. Except that on this night she was very relaxed, not frightened as when we first met, and definitely clad in more clothes!

Instantly that scene of twenty years prior replayed in my mind. My son had a playdate at his friend Jason's house. I was divorced by this time and since I had custody only on weekends, I wasn't familiar with all his friends. On this day my ex-wife had asked me to pick him up. The only information I had was Jason's address.

I slowly drove down the street looking for the house. Seeing the gate open, I walked into the backyard, assuming I'd find the boys playing. Instead, clad only in a large towel, casually lying on a poolside chaise, was none other than my all-time favorite star, Barbra Streisand, complete with sunglasses and script in

BUDINO AL CIOCCOLATO (CHOCOLATE CREAM CUSTARD)
Serves 8

Caramel Base

½ cup sugar
2 tablespoons water
juice of ½ lemon

Chocolate Custard

2 cups milk or half-and-half
4 ounces (squares) semisweet chocolate
4 eggs
4 egg yolks
½ cup sugar

1) Preheat oven to 350°F. Select eight ½-cup metal or ovenproof custard molds.

2) To make the base: Combine the ½ cup sugar, water and lemon juice in a saucepan and bring to a boil. Let cook, bubbling, until the syrup becomes a light amber color. Take care not to let the syrup burn or it will be bitter.

3) To make custard: The moment the syrup is ready, pour equal amounts of it quickly into the eight molds. Swirl the syrup around so that is covers the bottom of each mold. Let cool at room temperature.

4) Heat the milk with chocolate, stirring until chocolate dissolves.

5) Beat eggs, egg yolks and ½ cup sugar until thickened and smooth. Pour milk or cream mixture into the egg mixture and blend. Strain custard, skim and discard foam.

6) Ladle the custard into the prepared molds. Arrange the molds in a baking dish and pour boiling water around them. Place the dish in the oven and bake until the custard is set in the center, about 30 minutes.

7) Remove the custard molds and let cool. Unmold when ready to serve. ✑

CRÈME BRÛLÉE
Serves 6

2 cups whipping cream
4 well-beaten eggs
2 tablespoons sugar
light brown sugar

1) In a double boiler, heat the cream until hot.

2) In a bowl, beat the eggs and continue beating while you slowly pour in the hot cream. Return the mixture to the double boiler and stir in the 2 tablespoons of sugar.

3) Heat, stirring constantly, until the mixture thickens and the custard coats a spoon. Pour the mixture into buttered custard cups and chill for 12 hours or overnight.

4) Completely cover the top of each custard with ¼- to ⅓-inch layer of sieved, light brown sugar. Place the custard cups in a shallow pan. Put in a cold oven. Turn the heat to 250°F. and heat until the sugar is caramelized. ✑

hand. I remember thinking this was like a scene from a movie, when Barbra, who was rightfully startled, fearfully asked who I was. Following reassuring introductions and casual conversation, she called for my son. Out he came and off we went. That was the last time I had seen her.

Back at the stove, the class was preparing ingredients when Barbra volunteered to help. I asked her to chop cilantro. She chopped it in her own inimitable style: slowly and precisely. I suggested a professional way to chop which is simple and fast. Then I accidentally stepped on her foot. After graciously accepting my red-faced apologies, she watched my chopping demo, thanked me and proceeded to chop the cilantro her way.

The dinner was delicious and especially the dessert. I remember Barbra using her spoon to clean the plate, then licking the spoon to get the last bit. For me, that was the ultimate compliment.

When it came time to say goodbye, I gave her a kiss on the cheek, unsettling her Ben Franklin-style glasses. Realizing I was an unabashed fan, she was very gracious and giggled.

Later a friend of mine boasted about spending a fortune on tickets for one of her last concerts. He bragged about how fabulous the experience would be and asked if I wanted to go. I paused for a moment to give it some thought and heard myself reply, "I stepped on her foot, served her chocolate custard and kissed her." What more could I want? Needless to say, I declined, choosing to keep my special memories just the way they were. ✑

Budino al Cioccolato

FLAMBÉ BERRIES
Serves 4 to 6

3 heaping tablespoons sugar
½ cup water
1 pint fresh berries, washed and picked over
1 teaspoon fresh lemon juice
¼ cup brandy
1 quart ice cream

1) In a saucepan, heat the sugar and water over low heat, stirring constantly until the sugar dissolves. Add the berries, heat them through 2-3 minutes and stir in lemon juice.

2) Warm the brandy and slowly pour over the berries. Do not stir! Ignite and spoon over scoops of ice cream. ✐

Choosing a mango is a lot like selecting a kiwi or avocado – it should be soft to the touch but not mushy. Considering that mangos are a heavy fruit, the end result of this recipe is a light and delicate dessert.

MANGO-LIME MOUSSE
Serves 6-8

5 pounds ripe mangos (about ½ pound each), peeled, pitted and coarsely chopped
1½ cup fresh lime juice
½ cup superfine granulated sugar
1 envelope unflavored gelatin
¼ cup cold water
2 egg whites at room temperature
pinch of salt
½ cup chilled heavy whipping cream
lime slices or mint sprigs for garnish

1) In a blender, puree the mangos with the lime juice. Transfer the puree to a bowl and add the sugar.

2) In a saucepan, sprinkle the gelatin over the cold water and let it soften, about 10 minutes. Over low heat, stir the gelatin until dissolved. Let cool. Stir the gelatin into the mango puree.

3) With a mixer, beat the egg whites with the salt to hold soft peaks. In a chilled bowl, beat the cream until it holds stiff peaks and fold it into the egg whites. Gently fold the mixture into the mango puree.

4) Divide the mousse among individual dishes or stemware. Allow the mousse to chill about 3 hours. Serve garnished with lime slices or a sprig of mint. ✐

We love to receive truffles as gifts, but rarely consider making them. I like to wrap them individually in elegant foil and place in a beautiful tin. Sometimes I place in paper candy cups and store flat in a gift box.

ORANGE CHOCOLATE TRUFFLES
Makes 2 dozen

1 cup (2 sticks) unsalted butter
1 pound semisweet chocolate, chopped
6 egg yolks
⅓ cup orange liqueur, preferably Grand Marnier
cocoa powder, chopped nuts or coconut for coating

1) Melt the butter in the top of a double boiler over simmering water. Add the chocolate, stirring until melted and smooth.

2) In a bowl, whisk the yolks. Stir a few spoonfuls of the hot chocolate mixture into the yolks and then stir the yolk mixture into the chocolate mixture. Cook, stirring constantly, for about 4 minutes, or until a thermometer reaches 160°F.

3) Remove the chocolate from the double boiler and pour it into a bowl. Allow the mixture to cool to room temperature, for about 45 minutes, stirring occasionally.

4) Gradually add the orange liqueur, whisking constantly. Cover the chocolate and refrigerate for at least 8 hours or overnight.

5) With cold hands, quickly roll teaspoonfuls (or larger if you prefer) of the chocolate mixture into balls. The chocolate will be firm when you scoop it from the bowl, but will mold easily. Roll the truffles in your choice of coatings, such as cocoa powder, finely chopped nuts or coconut before placing in paper candy cups or wrapping individually in foil. Store in the refrigerator. ✐

To the
"Taste bud Delight
DUDE"
Love,

GUY.
GRUB.

Nick,
You know I love
you man. I love
your food when
I think days it all!
xxoo

Much love
George,

Elizabeth Taylor

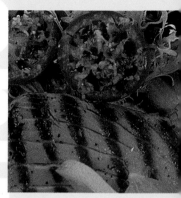

Food photography by Tom Paul

Candid photos of Nick Grippo and his friends and clients by Tom DeSimone and Nick Grippo, except as noted:

Elizabeth Taylor and Nick Grippo (pages 17, 18 and 20) by Robert Landau.

Johnny Mathis (page 30) by David Vance.

Nick Grippo and Ed Begley, Jr. (pages 32 and 34) by Tom Paul.

Cindy Williams's wedding party (page 39) by Tom Paul.

Carol Burnett and Elizabeth Taylor (page 50) by Chen Sam.

Nancy Reagan (page 56); used by permission of Mrs. Ronald Reagan.

Beach party (page 57) by Tom Paul.

Nick Grippo, Penny Marshall and Carrie Fisher (page 83) by Carol Claus.

Patrick Swayze and Nick Grippo (page 108) by Tom Paul.

Vicki! photo (page 114) by Tom Queally; courtesy of EyeMark Entertainment.

Cover of PLAYBILL on page 103 is used by permission. PLAYBILL® is a registered trademark of Playbill, Inc., N.Y.C. All rights reserved.

To find the same delicious foods Nick Grippo uses for his catered parties, e-mail him at nickgrippo@earthlink.net or call the following suppliers named in this book:

Emil's Swiss Pastry (310.277.1114) for fine custards and pastries.

Nate 'N' Al (310.274.0101) for fine deli meats, including Nick's favorite hot dogs.

Brown's Bakery (818.766.3258) for fine breads.

Jaqki's Cake Creations (818.769.4967) for fine wedding cakes.

HoneyBaked Hams (800.854.5995) for fine hams.

As I said earlier, I love all things associated with food. Especially the people. In fact, I'd be hard pressed to say which I like more: discovering a new recipe or making a new friend. That's why I started my newsletter. It's how I keep in touch with fans about new dishes I've created, while dishing out tips and perhaps telling a tale or two. If you'd like to receive my newsletter or have discovered a fabulous recipe you'd like to share, or want to know more about my catering services and gift baskets (yes, I travel!), write to me at Nick Grippo Catering, P.O. Box 9951, North Hollywood, California 91609-1951, or send e-mail to me at nickgrippo@earthlink.net.

Until then, I hope you've enjoyed my book — it's my first, you know, so I'd love to hear how much you like it.

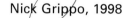

Nick Grippo, 1998

We wish to thank our mothers Frances Grippo and Thelma Covner, for instilling our love of cooking. Thanks to Irwin Russo, Peter Mitchell, Laurie Deans, Wendy Schneider, Brenda Koplin and Attica Locke for their eagle eyes; Rochell Goodrich Linker for encouragement; and Bruno Chiaruttini and Pat Cusick for the introduction to Angel City Press.

Thanks also to Tom Paul and Tom DeSimone for their photography over the years, Dave Matli for his inspired art direction, and Paddy Calistro and Scott McAuley at Angel City Press for their enthusiastic support of this project. And thanks, too, to Johnna Levine.